FIERCELY YOU

God, guts, glitter and glamour for the female entrepreneur

Gretchen Barocio

FIERCELY YOU

ISBN: 0692621822
ISBN 13: 9780692621820
Library of Congress Control Number: 2016902678
Fiercely You, Puyallup, WA

For more information: please visit www.thegirlpreneur.com or email infothegirlpreneur@gmail.com

HEELS PUBLISHING

For every girl and woman that may think they don't have what it takes. You do. There is nothing more real than the power manifested in your mind.

INTRODUCTION

I truly believe that one of the greatest powers, yet greatest destroyers in this world, is the power of the mind. I see it everywhere. In the work place, on social media and anywhere else the mind can be bound. We live in a day in age where we are so quick to medicate the issue rather than seek a cure. Not only about who we are, but what we've been created to be.

I am going to get so real in this book, that if someone decides to stop reading, that's okay. That person probably isn't ready to hear the truth like I am going to tell it when it comes to being an entrepreneur. I am a big believer in being real.

Let's face it, the world is crazy place today. We are bombarded by so many things telling us what we should be, what we should be doing, how we should dress, what we should be eating, where we should be working, what career path we should be on, and the like. It's mind numbing when you really think about it.

Did you know that the average human makes up to 35,000 choices a day? 35,000! That is insane when you break it down, so it's no wonder we live in a state of confusion all the time. It's no wonder it's easy to lose sight of what is really important. We forget to keep the main thing, the main thing.

Far too many people are stuck focusing on the negative aspects of life that they forget to live the positive life that God intended for us to live. Joyce Meyer even says herself, "We need to enjoy every day living."

So why is that so hard? I truly believe it is because we lack living a "fiercely you" lifestyle. We are so afraid of what the world will think when we are in pursuit of our passions and what God specifically designed us for, better known as the calling on our lives, that we succumb to the belief that we will never amount to more than what we believe we are. I spent twelve years in corporate America and not once was there a day that went by when someone asked the question, "how's it going," and the response was a sarcastic "living the dream." I knew there was no way they were "living the dream. If anything they were living a nightmare.

But the part that I found so crazy, so absurd, was that (myself included) if "living the dream was really living a nightmare, why in the world did we keep coming back every single day? Why do we continue to show up every day to a job or return to environments we can't stand?

More specifically, why was I showing up every single day to a job I couldn't stand and not enjoying every day life? Simple. Because I wasn't living a Fiercely You lifestyle. It was more comfortable to stay where I was and be completely miserable than it was to get off my rear and make a change. And change can be scary, but as I started to live more of a fierce lifestyle, it became scarier to continue to live as I was in a job I hated. I felt like a puppet every day, and I wasn't able to enjoy every day life because I was at the beck and call of everyone else.

I still don't have everything figured out, and that's just me being real. But here is what I will tell you. Once I started living fiercely, going after the call on my life and refusing to settle for anything less, life slowly started to get better as I progressed to the other side. Was the struggle real? One hundred percent. Was it hard? Absolutely. Was it worth the change? Definitely.

So, let's talk about who am I and why I wrote this book.

About six months ago, I started a blog called #THE-GIRLPRENEUR (www.thegirlpreneur.com). It actually wasn't anything that I had planned on doing, but I worked through it and created it with the help of my fabulous life coach, Cara Alwill Leyba. It was a way for me to voice my frustrations, be transparent and be 100%, unapologetically and authentically me. Just as God intended me to be.

Twelve years in the corporate arena had taken its toll on me and I needed an outlet to be able to be fiercely me. It was a way for me to be able to connect with female entrepreneurs and talk about one of the elements of life I am super passionate about as well, *business.* I speak best when I am writing, so I figured, why not? As I began writing, people would reach out to me on social media, people I had never met, and I would get responses like, "holy cow, it's like you read my mind" or "it's like you're inside my brain because I thought the exact same thing." As someone who has struggled with depression and anxiety for years, always in paid-to-perform positions, I always felt inadequate throughout my life. I never felt like I was good enough. That's just the real truth. Always striving for the next promotion, seeking affirmation in all the wrong places and allowing the corporate world (specifically) to validate me. Then I thought, well, I know if I have struggled with all of this and have felt like this, I know there are other people out there, women in particular, who have felt and feel the same way. I want others to know that you can live a Fiercely You lifestyle and not be ashamed about the way God hard wired you. I felt trapped for a long time, so the last thing I want is for others to make that same mistake.

I know what it's like feeling like you are in the shadows. I know what it's like feeling like you don't measure up to society's standards. I know what it's like feeling left out. I know what it's like feeling like you are the only one who sees the dream. I know what it's like having people talk about you and shun you behind your back and then turn right around, look you in the eye and give you a hug. I know what it's like when you are struggling with something so deep you are ashamed to share it with anyone else. I know because I have experienced it all (and then some).

I felt a complete conviction from the Holy Spirit that the only way I was going to reach the masses on a deep level was to be transparent myself. I have also included nine absolutely fantastic interviews from some of the fiercest of females who have had a tremendous impact on my life in one way or another over the years. They are leaders in their industry and have shared some of the similar struggles and have now been willing to share those with you as well.

I've learned in my twelve-year business career that it is tough to be Fiercely You because there will always be someone or something trying to take you down. But you can't be afraid of the opposition, especially as a Jesus girl. You can't allow the enemy to derail you from what you know is the call on your life. Most people who know me well know I am a quote person. One of my absolute favorite quotes (and I say it all the time) is, "There are two important days in one's life. The day they are born and they day they find out why." It is the total truth. How many of you can honestly say there is a significant amount of time that has been wasted living a life that is not Fiercely You?

It's time to change that. So, get your fabulous Louboutins on, get a pen and paper, grab a Starbucks and get ready to learn how to become Fiercely You.

CHAPTER 1

YOU CAN'T HIDE FROM YOURSELF

"The most exciting, challenging and significant relationship of all is the one you have with yourself."

–Carrie Bradshaw

Yes I know this quote is from *Sex and the City* but I absolutely love it because there is definitely a truth to it and here is why. Did you know that in a recent case study that when a group of people were asked the question "do you like yourself?" that a staggering 57% of the group responded "no?"

Yikes! And yes, once upon a time, I was one of those people. It is a challenge to have a relationship with yourself. I hid from myself for years. And worse off, I hid from who I was in Jesus. I am absolutely convinced that it is easy to fall into that trap of the 57% with all the things we have in the world today to provide us, as I call it, superficial validation.

Superficial Validation versus Jesus Validation

Take social media, for example. How often do we find ourselves on social media searching for validation in how many likes or followers we have? I am about to get even more real. How many times do *you* let that affect your train of thought? You can't tell me that we don't seek validation from social media in some fashion because I am going to call myself out and admit that, yes, I did, too, at one point. How ridiculous is that? Don't get me wrong. Social media is an amazing platform for business, entrepreneurship, connecting, networking, getting your message out there and being heard, fostering relationships, etc. If it weren't for social media, I wouldn't have been able to build the platform I have now. But when we start to allow it to overtake how we view ourselves and how we treat ourselves then we haven't kept the main thing the main thing. You can't hide from who you are.

Understand that you were fearfully and wonderfully made. I want you to really get that. I say that because it took me a lifetime to understand that. I remember as a kid, growing up and hearing that phrase. I remember thinking, too, *yeah, well, Beyonce, Joyce Meyer, Oprah, Christine Caine, etc. all have their thing going on so I guess I won't amount to much. There is no way I can make a way for myself in the business world, especially as a Jesus girl, so rather than work on me and for myself, I will just go work for someone else.* And I buried my head in the sand for twelve years! Did God waste that time?

Absolutely not. But because I hid from myself, God took me on a journey of growth that I had to go on in order to get to the other side.

Asking the question

I want you to ask yourself candidly right now, what is holding you back and keeping you hidden from yourself? Is it a job? Perhaps a toxic relationship? Maybe even yourself? I get it's a tough question to ask, but it's a necessary question to ask. If you want to live and lead a fierce life, you have to get real with yourself because no one else is going to do it for you. And the problem doesn't stop there. When we refuse to get real with ourselves, we, in turn, allow the devil to get a foot hold on our life where he has no business residing. We start to allow small, tiny, what may seem like minuscule things creep into our life and then before you know it, you start to believe those lies to be truths. Furthermore, I am convinced that this is one of the biggest reasons, if not the biggest reason, that depression plagues the world to the capacity it does today. I speak with more women battling depression and how it affects their business than any other topic.

Here in the U.S., a major depressive disorder affects approximately 14.8 million American adults each year. While a major depressive disorder can develop at any age, the median age at onset is 32. And to top it all off, major depressive disorders are more prevalent in women than men. (Dang, ladies! We have some serious work to do!)

The Ugly Truth

Here is where it really starts getting real. Back in early 2011, I was at one of the worst spots in my life. I had just had my second baby, I was struggling with balancing a full time corporate career, my other older child, a full time working husband, all while trying to be a wife with a major health issue with my reproductive system. There were days I felt like the most inadequate mom because all I would want to do is sleep. I felt guilty because I was away from my babies Monday through Friday, and felt even worse because I didn't want to be a stay-at-home mom like most of my friends were. I longed to have a thriving career. I was so totally irrational some days, and God bless my ever-loving husband for putting up with my array of crap. Sometimes, my husband would leave with the kids and go stay with his parents because I was so out of balance.

I remember taking myself to a doctor to find out "what was wrong with me." Aside from what I am sure was partially due to a significant lack of sleep, I felt so empty. I felt lost. I remember walking into the doctor's office and telling myself, "Gretchen, this isn't you. You can turn around and leave. This is embarrassing anyway to have to be here admitting you have depression."

Still, I went into the doctor's office and sat there over an hour with her while she took me down the path that turned into a series of questions. I distinctly remember one of the questions being, "Have you ever thought about ending your life?"

I burst into tears because although I had never thought about ending my life, I thought about what life would be like if I just weren't here. I had thoughts of, "Well, if I were to die suddenly, then my husband and children would then at least be able to take the life insurance, pay off all the debt and be financially set."

I was a total mess. How in the world was I going to lead a successful career if I couldn't even lead myself? I was totally hiding from who I was. I was allowing my circumstances to dictate how I conducted myself, how I acted toward my family, how I ran my business and, ultimately, the circumstances ran me down. I allowed the enemy to get a foot hold in my life that he had no business being in. That day I left the doctor's office with a prescription for anti-depression medication and to this day, I have the medication still sitting in my medicine cabinet. Completely untouched. Never took one pill. I keep them there in my medicine cabinet as a daily reminder of what I was able to beat. I was able to beat the depression, over time of course, because I got real with myself. I stopped hiding from who I was and who God created me to be. Once I stopped hiding from who I was, my business started to really take off. There is only one of you, so embrace you fully and understand that God did not create you to fit in.

You're probably saying, "Yeah, well, Gretchen, you don't understand how bad it really is for me." I might not know your full situation, but I will say this, and I can say this with complete confidence and conviction. I have been on the verge of bankruptcy and have had sleepless nights of wondering how I was going to put food on the table or keep the lights on. I've lost loved ones unexpectedly. I've been shunned from a church and asked not to speak truth (twice). I've been demoted in the corporate arena twice. I've had major health issues that put me in the hospital six times. I also have a son who is a high-functioning autistic child. To top it off, I've been battling depression for over a decade now. Believe me, the struggle is real. We all have one. But that is where we have to cling to the hope of Jeremiah 29:11 (AMP) in that, " 'For I know the plans *and* thoughts that I have for you,' says the Lord, 'plans for peace *and* well-being and not for disaster, to give you a future and a hope."

Fiercely You secret number one: You are fearfully and wonderfully made.

There is no reason not to love yourself as you are right now, right where you are at. That is the beauty of the journey. Just like peaks and valleys in the geographical sense, you will have the peaks and valleys in life and in your business. You have to embrace them. It's what makes you who you are. And there is no shame or reason for you to hide from that. *When you hide from yourself, you miss the unbelievable opportunity for growth.* Write that down, highlight it, stick somewhere where you can see that daily. Seriously.

John C. Maxwell, one of my absolute favorite leaders and authors in the industry, says it best. "If you are not growing, you are dying." So don't limit yourself by hiding from who you are. Have the guts to be who God created you to be. So you might lose a little glitter on the crown as you move through your journey, and your Louboutins might even get scuffed up a bit, but don't deny yourself the opportunity to grow into who you really are.

A model, an army wife, a mom and business owner

So as promised, here we go with fierce female number one. Her name is Veronica Kelly. She's someone I actually met in church. I taught her two younger girls in my kids ministry class. We got to talking one day randomly about business and girly things and I was just enamored with her story. From there, we are pretty inseparable. A former army wife, model and successful makeup artist, where her most recent accolade is having worked for the top elite at IMATS LA (International Makeup and Artist Trade Show), learning from the best of the best. Grab some coffee and get ready for this fierce female and her story of success to the top.

Social Media

Instagram: @ver_kelly
YouTube: VeronicaKellyMUA
Facebook: VeronicaKellyMUA
Periscope: @verkelly
Twitter: VerKellyMUA
Website: www.verkelly.com
Nerium: www.verkelly.nerium.com

So tell us about yourself!

I am a Canadian immigrant, retired US Army Wife, US Army Mom and mom of four. My oldest son is twenty and is in the US Army, my youngest son is sixteen, my daughters are seven and five years old.

When did you realize you were born to be an entrepreneur in the make-up and beauty industry?
That's almost two questions in one. An entrepreneur raised me, so I really didn't know there was any other way of life other than being an entrepreneur. I was fortunate enough to have a successful Christian entrepreneur as a role model, mentor and Dad. I went to an arts high school and majored in visual arts and minored in business. Seeing my love for both, my Dad would often ask for my input on his marketing projects and trips to the printers. I loved the psychology behind marketing – especially how it applied in the beauty industry. When I was in college, I was discovered by Shok Models in Toronto, Canada. I modeled with them for a few years and loved it. I soaked up as much knowledge as possible. If there was a profession that I could have as a soul mate, it's definitely modeling! Back then, there were no digital cameras, editing programs or filters. You had to know your craft well in order to excel in your field. I was lucky to learn the tricks of the trade during that time. As a model, you had to know your angles, your colors, and how to elicit emotions using your body to sell products. You had to know how to use your environment and develop your creativity. As time went on, my life took another direction, but my passion for the beauty and make-up industry never ended.

As an army wife, how did you deal with the pressures of moves, children, your business, being a wife, etc?
Listen, being a US Army wife is no joke. You are often left behind, isolated, and expected to thrive in unhealthy

environments. Your incredible sacrifices are overlooked, you're told you have no value and that your life, goals, and dreams don't matter. You're laughed at and treated like a burden or a stereotype. And just when you think you can't possibly feel any worse, you're blindsided as you observe your children go through being treated the same way. You feel helpless and infuriated when they're treated like an outcast or a "military brat." My children and I have given up more for this country than most of its own citizens. The pain makes you question just how long you can endure your marriage and keep it together as a military family. (On a total side note, did you know that more spouses than soldiers have PTSD?)

I have definitely felt the pressure at times in my life. I will get more into my story in a future question, but the businesses have been vital for me in staying focused on the bigger picture. It's easy to get sucked in to the military bubble where the military becomes your whole lifestyle. I was able to use the businesses as a tool to keep my family focused on life outside and after the military.

All of my businesses have provided an opportunity to create a sense of family by working together on projects, and celebrating all our hard work and victories. They've been an outlet for creativity and growth. It's been a safe place for each of my children to share and foster their unique talents, to voice their ideas and learn that they matter, have value and learn that they can contribute and make a difference. These values are important to learn at home, because most children are not learning that in the world.

How do you see yourself as Jesus sees you?
The beauty industry is cruel. It plays on your insecurities. It's demanding, aggressive, threatening at times, and there's a lot of pressure to do things that you may not agree with. When I started my beauty blog, I did so at the request of my friends and family. Being an immigrant and committed to the US Army, my loved ones lived all over the world. The Internet was a great place to teach make-up in a central location accessible twenty-four hours a day. I was not in it to make money, just to share my knowledge with those who asked for help. The blog grew into a bigger platform with an Instagram account and a YouTube channel.

There are many women doing the same thing I do. Sex appeal sells. It's what gets you followers and viewership, which in turn creates opportunity for sponsorships, endorsements, affiliations, contracts, etc. My challenge has always been to represent Christ, as a person in the beauty industry. I try to remember that he sees me as his daughter. As such, I try to represent myself and be an example of what is elegant and classy. I do not dress provocatively, or promote a partying lifestyle. There's no profanity and I do not post things that put others down.

The challenge, however, comes when I see a new account grow faster than mine because they offer all the things I don't. There are times when I wrestle with whether or not to dress daringly or pose suggestively to try to get ahead. I question whether the level of success I would like will come. I flirt with shortcuts. But I have to hold true to what I believe. I think there are so many girls and women who are craving a real example of a Proverbs 31 woman. I may or may not be that example, but I want my social media accounts to be a safe place for females of all ages to visit, be encouraged and feel good about themselves with what they are learning on my sites.

But listen, y'all, I am a REAL woman, with four REAL children and a husband that has gone to fight a REAL war several times – you're going to see me post a picture of a Vertini or two. It just is what it is.

Do you have a mission statement, and if so, what is it? How did you come up with it?

In 2015, the church we attended while living in Washington State created a yearly theme called "Expect More." The idea was not to put human limits on a supernatural God, but to expect more from Him and from ourselves. What God can do and what He has in store will always be beyond our human expectations. We were then given two business-card sized cards to write our biggest God-sized expectations for the year. One of the cards was for us to keep, the other was to anonymously write our expectations down and post it on the sanctuary walls where we could revisit them as needed throughout the year. To this day, I keep my card in my wallet as a reminder and mission statement, if you will, to keep me on track when I feel lost.

"Lord, please use me to empower women. To make them feel strong and confident. To make them fearless to experience more of life. Give me the ability to be a good teacher and be Your example."

What inspires you the most in your entrepreneurial journey?

What inspires me most is that my entrepreneurial spirit is a gift from God, a tool to be used to strengthen our relationship. I am in constant awe of the places God brings me. Never in my wildest dreams could I have dreamed up the opportunities that have opened for me. I love that I am on this journey with Him. I love seeing the linear effect of obedience and blessings. It's actually more of a cyclical effect: obedience, blessings, more opportunity. I find growth in the discomfort of more opportunity. I think God calls you out of your comfort zone in that area. And it cycles back to obedience in your discomfort, then the blessings pour out and the cycle continues. There are so many times I catch myself saying, "Is this my real life right now?" I have grown into the person He is maturing me into. My journey intertwines with countless other lives that I have to ability to affect. And knowing that, I try my best to be a positive and encouraging force in the world. I hope one day to see the bigger picture of how our stories are all woven together.

What fears do you have and how have you (or do you) overcome them?

I have a fear of wasting resources. Of spending time, energy and money irresponsibly. I fear that failure lessens the abundance by which people will pour into you. Almost like the boy who cried wolf. As a military wife with an entrepreneurial spirit, my businesses have always had to be portable. And that has not always been an option. This part of my story may be lengthy. Grab a snack, take a bathroom break and then get comfy. Because seriously what I'm about to tell you is something I can't even make up!

Before I married my husband, I had started a candle company back in Canada. When I moved from Canada to the USA, I transferred my business license to Texas. I had several customers there and had even gotten my merchandise on the shelves of some local stores. During that time, I became pregnant with our third child. Very shortly thereafter, my husband deployed to Iraq for the second time, leaving me with two children, a child on the way, a business to run and my immigration status up in the air. We were forced to move off Post into a new house due to regulations regarding amount of kids versus bedrooms in government housing. So that's how I ended up buying my first house. Halfway through his deployment, he was allowed to take ten days leave. He ended up arriving back home in Texas an hour before my daughter was born. From the hospital, we went home to the house I had bought while he was away, which we were still in the process of unpacking. A few days after my daughter was born, my mother passed away from cancer. I could not go back to Canada to attend her funeral because my immigration wasn't finalized and the Army would not allow my husband to stay home from deployment a few days longer for me to make arrangements. So, back to war he went and I was left to figure out the rest. Alone.

When he came home from Iraq six months later, the military decided to move us to Georgia and I had to transfer my business license again (plus the actual business itself. The Army will move your household goods, but not a personal business.) Customers lose faith in you when you aren't stable in business, so I lost many customers from that move. Plus, I had lost my mom who was one of the main sources of support in my life. And since we're tracking, I'm now moving from Texas to Georgia with three children, two cats, two cars, and a moving van we rented to move the business. A moving company is trailing us with our household goods and oh yeah, I'm now eight months pregnant with baby number four. (Lord have mercy). I set up my candle business for a third time, this time in Georgia. I had baby number four and a month later my father died unexpectedly. He took his own life, heartbroken from the loss of my mother. Thankfully, I was far enough into the immigration process (although it was not finalized) that I was able to go home for that.

My husband was feeling the pressure by all the responsibilities in our life and asked me to get another job. I started working for a homebuilder during the day and went to real estate school at night. Meanwhile, my husband was in and out of the state on training missions. I'm happy to say not only was I one of the only ones to pass the real estate school itself but, I was THE only one to pass the state exam! Being a realtor, you are your own business. So here starts my second ongoing business where I am relying on friends and family for support, business and referrals.

If you're tracking my Georgia experience, I've moved halfway across the country by car while pregnant, unpacked a house, unpacked and set up a candle-making business, had my fourth baby, my father died traumatically and unexpectedly, I'm working full time and going to school at night and my husband is around sporadically. Something had to give with all this stress, and you know what did? My heart. I had a stress-induced heart attack. Time to call both candle and real estate clients and tell them I was out of business....again.

The Army sent my husband a few states away to a school for three months. When he returned, they thought it best to move us to Washington. And by the time we got to Washington, I was overwhelmed. We had four children, a cross-country move, another unexpected immediate deployment to Afghanistan and my oldest son had a near fatal accident. I was completely alone in another new place and something had to give. *Ver Kelly the entrepreneur* needed a break, so a sabbatical was in order. Although it's not in my nature to sit still for long. And since my real estate license didn't transfer to our new state, I wasn't able to pick that back up.

While home managing our family during the Afghanistan deployment, I decided after the prompting of friends and family to start a make-up blog. I did it for fun, but very quickly fell in love with it. And if you're tracking, here comes business number three. Once again, I was calling upon the support of friends almost exclusively. My parents had both passed away and my husband was gone. It's a lot to ask of people after they've supported your previous business attempts. This time, I didn't have any expectations. I just used it as an outlet for creativity and fun and to create connections with people online.

When my network marketing opportunity came along, I felt like this was the fourth time in a decade I had asked my friends and extended family to support a new venture. It was not easy. But I thought since I had been actively helping them with make-up and skincare advice with my blog, that this would be an easy transition into a new venture. I absolutely loved the products the company was behind and already had a platform to share it. However, the enthusiasm from my loved ones was definitely not there.

As I wrestled with that, I realized that God had gathered all of my weaknesses with this company. Nerium, my company, is a turnkey business. There's really no entrepreneurship involved. The work has been done for you. You just get out there and promote a brand. To this point, I had become quite skilled at all aspects of owning your own company except for the network marketing portion. God has used this as a tool for me to develop those skills and put into my life the right people to help me do it. And that puts me smack dab in the middle of the uncomfortable obedience part of the cycle. And you know what follows that? BLESSINGS! So watch out, there are some major blessings to be shared soon, because I'm in some major discomfort!

What advice do you have for women who struggle with hiding from who they are?

First of all, you are not alone in your feelings. BUT, you are meant for so much more! You do not have to have it all figured out to get started! Business and life are organic; they develop over time, always moving, changing and growing. There is absolutely no way to map out the entire journey.

Just get started. If jumping right in seems too overwhelming, make small goals – even if they are not related to what you want to get into. Each time you reach them you build more and more confidence in yourself and your abilities. You are absolutely not limited by anything. There is nothing in this world that you cannot learn. The secret to success is motion. You have to get out there and actually DO something, not sit around and dream about it.

What is the number one thing you have learned in your journey as a Jesus girl and business woman?

Currently, I'm working on overcoming the guilt of being financially successful. Somewhere throughout my life, I got the message that having money and success as a Jesus girl was a bad thing. I thought Christians were poor mostly by choice and that you are being disobedient to God by keeping a surplus in your bank account. I turned to Michael Key, Emmy award-winning make-up artist and the editor-in-chief of Make-Up Artist Magazine and executive producer of the International Make-Up Artist Trade Show (IMATS) for advice. Michael Key is a very successful Christian businessman who regularly shares his musical talent and love of the guitar via his church band. His advice to me was to tithe regularly. By being humble and obedient to God, He will bless you beyond measure and continue to give you opportunities to grow and serve others. I have read several books on how to create and run a Christian-value-based organization. I regularly remind myself that although I am the president of my company, God is truly the CEO of my life. The decisions and actions in my business need to glorify Him and provide value and service to others.

What is one thing you do every single day?
I am working on spending time with God every day. Being intentional about reading His word and praying and giving him the start of my day. Some days, finding the time is difficult with having four children. I'm also addicted to my phone and I like to turn the morning alarm off and check my social media. I decided to see if I could turn my weakness into a strength by finding a short daily devotion that would be accessible first thing in the morning. I found this amazing free daily devotional written by Bill Gothard from the Institute in Basic Life Principals called *Daily Success.* It is a series of 343 daily e-mails that are sent for 49 consecutive weeks. The program focuses on one commandment of Christ each week. It's e-mailed at 6am EST. It dives into the *Commands of Christ* and explores how to learn and apply them. There are great examples of how to live out your daily life supported by scripture from the KJV. It has really transformed my days by starting my morning with Christ.

How do you stay disciplined in your business?
There are certain skill sets that you develop over time. Discipline is one of them. And discipline in itself waxes and wanes. It's easy to go full bore when you start a project or business. The ideas are flowing easily and you feel like you need to get it all out before you forget. There's high energy and expectations. There is no taste of failure. It can sometimes be easy to get burnt out in the beginning. Finding a rhythm that works for you and plugging into a like-minded culture is a must. Like-minded people understand your ups and downs. They appreciate your journey and will have the experience to give you the encouragement you need.

Also, take advantage of the tools created by the experts who came before you. Whether it's learning materials, books, webinars, planners, systems, and the like. These individuals have perfected their craft. Give them a chance to help you. Let people do the jobs they were created to do instead of trying to do it all yourself. It's easier to stay disciplined when you have a system to follow.

Coffee Thoughts:

1. What is one way you can validate yourself in Jesus' eyes and apply that to your business?

____
____
____
____
____

2. What is one thing you can do to start surrounding yourself with like-minded people?

____
____
____
____
____

3. What is one thing holding you back from being who God created you to be?

____
____
____
____
____

CHAPTER 2

IT'S JUST PLAIN DETERMINATION.

"I am not what happened to me. I am what I chose to become."

–Carl Gustav Jung.

Time to say "goodbye" to being the victim

I love this quote by Carl Gustav Jung. Seriously, love it. You have to say 'goodbye' to the victim mentality. Nobody wants to be around that. For years, I toiled over whether to quit my corporate job or not. I would *constantly* come home and complain about how much I hated my boss(es) or how boring a meeting was. I actually made Starbucks runs sometimes with some of my colleagues just so we could get out of the office and complain about all the corporate bureaucracy we couldn't stand. Childish, I know. But I played a victim. It was always "woe is me."

The reality? Corporate America really was a tough place to be. It was not a "user friendly" environment. The only using that took place in the environment was simply the use of people as numbers to get a job done so that at the end of the day, the bottom line was met. I get it. That's the corporate world. Day after day, week after week, year after year, people work away at a job that they hate, but they don't do *anything* about it. Why? Fear..... plain and simple. Most people are as determined to complain and drone on about how much they hate their jobs just as much as they are determined to *not* do a darn thing about it. I was one of them, too (let me just call myself to the carpet first).

Our realities

The harsh reality? I was so miserable at my job, so unhappy, so depressed, overworked, tired, angry, frustrated and empty that I almost drove my husband away. No joke. There were days he questioned why in the world he was even putting up with my array of personalities, complaints and frustrations. It landed us in marriage counseling....twice. I spent over a decade living in a dark depression because I was not determined enough to get out of it, although I didn't know it at the time. I have worked with countless men and women in the same corporate world who all say the exact same thing. And guess what? They are determined to stay where they are at and they don't even realize it.

Here is what you really need to get. You become what you believe. You have the power and inclination to change whatever in your life needs to be changed. You just have to get violently fierce with it. Yes, *violently* fierce. The enemy will do whatever he can to hold you back. I love in Joyce Meyer's book *Battlefield of the Mind* (which by the way I highly recommend picking that up and reading it yourself if you haven't yet), she talks about "resisting the devil at his onset." All of those things I listed above are not of God, they are of the enemy. You have to get that. If you are undetermined to do anything to change your life, the enemy has you right where he wants you. You're not a threat to significant life change. You are not a threat to furthering the kingdom. The moment you feel fear in taking a leap faith, the moment you feel depressed about a situation you are in, the moment you realize you're going down a path of complaining and griping, stop yourself and resist it at the enemy's onset. Get violently fierce with it. You are a daughter of the most High King. You aren't what's happened to you, you are who you've become, and more importantly, who you were created in Christ to be.

The Bible is specific when it comes to determination. Galatians 6:9 says (AMP), "Let's not grow weary or become discouraged in doing good, for at the proper time we will reap, if we do not give in." I gave in so much, more times than I can count. Although I can't and refuse to beat myself up over it anymore, I now recognize it when I see it and make the determination to change it. It took me twelve years. I can't and won't stand for the enemy robbing me of any piece of my life that is designed exactly the way the Lord intended. It might take you a shorter period of time or it might take you a longer period of time to make the necessary changes in your life that are needed. But if you are flat out fiercely determined to do it, it *will* happen.

What do I do with that now?

So how does this apply to your business and a serious life change? You have to have an unwavering desire to change it. I speak with a lot of female entrepreneurs that get caught up in the comparison game. They think that just because someone did something in a shorter time frame than they are doing it in, it automatically makes them a failure. Couldn't be further from the truth. It comes down to determination. And let's be real. Comparison is ugly. It serves no purpose. If I compared my journey to anyone else's in the entrepreneurial world, the enemy would have me right where he wants me. Pinned down and feeling hopeless again. I had to learn to become extremely comfortable with being uncomfortable. Nothing really worth having comes from comfort zones.

If you can't stand that job you're in now, do something about it and stop worrying what other people will think. If you want change in your life, go after it. *God did not intend for you to live your life undetermined.* He didn't send His only son to die for us so that we could live in misery and have no joy. You have get so fierce with yourself and who God created you to be, that more often times than not, people are going to think you are crazy. They won't be able to see your vision and the call you have on your life because they are determined to stay where they are at. Like I said before, nothing really worth having comes from comfort zones.

Fiercely You secret number two: The *will* and the *why* must be bigger than the *how* and the *when*.

If you have the determined will and your why is unshakeable, then the how and when won't matter. I spoke a few months back with a phenomenal woman by the name of Deanna Stull, Chief Experience Officer at Coachville (one of the best coaching schools in the country) and she said it so well: "We shouldn't look at what we went through as wasted time, but what we needed to go through in order to get to other side." She is absolutely correct. There is no wasted time in a journey. It's about the process. All that matters is that your determined will and your unshakeable why stay intact.

A mom of five and an international network marketing sensation.

Here is an interview I did with one of my absolute favorite "mompreneurs" in the network marketing industry, Jennifer Johnson. She is an amazing leader in her industry. She has five children, a husband and a thriving career as a Jesus girl and business woman. I think what inspired me the most about Jennifer is that she has five children! Seriously, sometimes I feel like I am dying with just my two and running my businesses. But her story, her struggles and her ability to persevere through it just drew me to her. And, of course, when I met her, I immediately connected with her on the working mom thing. Enjoy this fierce female's story. It definitely empowered me.

When did you realize you were you were an entrepreneur?

It was a progressive journey to the realization I was an entrepreneur. There were definitely those "ah-ha" moments along the way. When I was going to the University of Montana part-time while working full-time for an accounting firm, I saw how much they were paying me compared to how much they were charging my clients for my services. For the most part, I was responsible for scheduling my day, retaining my clients and getting referrals on my own. That was a huge light bulb for me. Also, I've never enjoyed having a boss or being told what to do. In fact, during one of my evaluations, I was told that because I was a woman, young and attractive, I would have to work harder to be taken seriously. I left my boss's office in tears but felt a huge surge of independence rise up in me. The idea of going out out my own and to be totally honest…proving that I could be successful without the traditional job, became a heartbeat I couldn't ignore. I fell in love with the freedom of calling my own shots and being 100% responsible for what I brought home.

When I began my network marketing career, it dawned on me that I finally found a profession where my healthy rebellion and stubbornness paid off! Being an entrepreneur takes grit and a resolve to never quit no matter what… which is completely against how our get-rich-quick society, as a whole, operates.

How did you deal with the pressures of life, children, your business, and being a wife, etc.?

On my knees! I only feel pressure in my life with all the hats I wear when I take my focus off of Christ and put it onto the world. What the world's expectations are…what my kids' friends' moms are doing…what my parents think I should do… the guilt of it never being good enough.

When my eyes are on Christ and I seek his guidance and perspective daily…the only expectation is that I do the best with what I have…that day! Easier said than done.

There is an ENORMOUS amount of pressure on moms today…to be everything to everyone. The moment I let go of the notion that I didn't have to be everything to everyone, I felt the pressure disappear.

How do you see yourself as Jesus sees you?
This is a tough one. I'd be lying if I didn't say it's been a struggle to make sure I see myself the way He sees me. After being abused as a child, I spent twenty years trying to find "me." The enemy would love nothing more than to skew how we see ourselves. It's easy to think you're worthless, destined to be just like your family and not capable of greatness. The enemy had a hay-day messing with my self-image for years. As a result, my natural human instinct is to beat myself up…thinking I will never measure up to Christ's standards, that He probably gets really tired watching me screw up over and over. But the beautiful part about being saved is that…I'm not saved because of what I do..or don't do…or how I do it. It's all about HIM!! Who HE is. What HE did for me. When I can keep that perspective, I can live loved. I can live in His GRACE! I love the grace of Christ…because I no longer have to live in condemnation, but freedom! Freedom to become the woman he has always destined me to be…because of what HE did for me! I love how Pastor Furtick says that not only is He the God of your successes, but He is the God in your pain, in your failure

and in your hurts. God knows what you went through or are going through... and he's just waiting for you to allow Him to accept His embrace!

Do you have a mission statement, and if so, what is it? How did you come up with it?
I am a confident woman who values family and honesty. I joyfully inspire others to believe in themselves by investing in them and showing them Christ's love.

This was the result of my training with David Byrd. Hearing him talk about your state of being....the things that matter most to you. I imagine this will evolve, but this has been my mission statement for three years!

What inspires you the most in your entrepreneurial journey?
Giving others hope and freedom by believing in them. I know what I've been able to accomplish and I know what I lack. I know what I've been through. If I can do it, everyone can accomplish AMAZING things... but sometimes they just need someone to believe in them. I'm here to be that person.

What fears do you have and how have you (or do you) overcome them?
I have actually thought about this and it terrifies me to no end. I fear losing my mind...like literally waking up one day and not being able to worship Jesus. Not being able to be changed by the words of the Bible. Not being

able to be inspired by people. Not being able to function mentally. Ironically, this fear is fought in the mind...in the same word...on my knees...trusting Him that He will protect my soul and my ability to continue to worship him forever!

What advice do you have for women who struggle with finding and holding onto their determined 'why' and unshakeable 'will'?
Give yourself permission to dream. Accept God's grace for you. So many women I meet do not feel comfortable establishing a *why* for themselves. They feel guilty, they feel like it's selfish. You were not put on this earth to feel lousy, intimidated, insecure, unsure and constantly needing affirmation. You were put here for a reason! To live a FULL, BOLD life! To reach your maximum potential! To influence and thrive. Not to follow and just survive. Allow yourself to believe and to develop a desire for greatness. If you see yourself the way God sees you, you will see a blank slate and he's holding the marker and wanting to write your story. He's just waiting for you to take the first step!

What is the number one thing you have learned in you journey as a Jesus girl in business woman?
You must have grit, integrity and a boldness like no other. But above all, you must seek Him in all of your choices. Everything I do is for His glory! If it doesn't shine a light on him....instead, maybe it will shine a light on me...then, I stay away from it. Everything is to shine a light on Him!!

What is one thing you do every single day?

I would love to say pray, workout and have sex! But…I'm all about being honest… So… I would say every day I ask him for help. Sometimes it's a beautiful prayer on my knees, sometimes it's through a clenched jaw and fists tight, sometimes it's a pleading through painfully salty tears that have rubbed my cheeks raw, sometimes it's in unison with my husband, sometimes it's in the middle of fight, sometimes it's an unadulterated child-like begging to make things right. But everyday…I ask Him for help.

How do you stay disciplined in your business?
I've tried to implement keystone habits. Those habits that lead to other habits. In my life, one discipline always leads to the next. If these disciplines are active, my business follows right in line. This doesn't mean I do them perfectly everyday…far from it… but this is my standard, what I strive for. And when I'm on…I'm absolutely unstoppable!

These are my daily keystone habits/disciplines:

- Quiet time/prayer time/time with Jesus
- Exercise
- Eating 5-6 times/day clean, healthy meals
- Spend 15 minutes with my husband
- Plan tomorrow before tomorrow begins.

Weekly:

- Sunday worshiping with my family
- Meal prepping
- Spend 1 evening with my husband
- Plan my week before the week begins.

Monthly:

- Spend 1 day with my husband
- Plan my month before the month begins
- Plan date nights with each child

When all of these habits are active, my mind, body and soul are ready for major productivity and focus to tackle the activities that are required to drive my business!

Coffee Thoughts:

1. What is one thing you can do every single day that better represents God?

____
____
____
____
____

2. What is one thing you have been determined to finish for so long and haven't yet? (Put a time line to the arrival "at the finish line" of that one thing.)

____
____
____
____
____

CHAPTER 3

CONFIDENCE VS. CONDEMNATION

"Condemnation without investigation is the height of ignorance."

–Albert Einstein

How true that is. Again, if you haven't figured it out by now, I am such a quote person. Another one of my favorites, and I am only including this one right out of the gate as well because it is too good *not* to:

> "Any fool can criticize, condemn and complain- and most fools do."
>
> *–Dale Carnegie.*

I am going to dive deep into this topic this chapter, so you better get your highlighter out and ready, slip off the Louboutins for a minute and get comfortable.

First, let me be transparent in saying that I lived with condemnation for years. And by years, I mean probably most of my life. And for no reason in particular other than, hindsight being 20/20, that the enemy was going to do whatever it took to bring me down. The enemy wants nothing more than to shove you in a corner and make you feel like your hopes and dreams are really out of reach, especially when it has to do with furthering your business and business of the kingdom. I get that all businesses are not geared toward promoting the Great Commission, but my life's call is business, the Great Commission and leading women out of depression and anxiety simply the way God led me out of it, both in my business life and my own personal life.

Doubt and disbelief

I had a good upbringing. I had no real cause to even feel condemnation. In fact, my husband teases me all the time because he says that I was the "social butterfly" in high school with friends, always into sports, always involved in some sort of student-government-type deal (which is the complete opposite of what he was like in school.) But what he failed to realize (my husband that is and quite possibly many others) is that I was seeking validation in all the wrong places. Like seriously, who even cares about high school now? And for the record, *validation is for parking only*. But I was seeking validation in all the wrong places at an early stage in life. I was always looking for the next performance metric to hit so I would get the recognition I needed to feel better about myself. I know……stuuuuuupid. So of course, it was only natural when that same sentiment crept in and spilled over into my twelve-year career in corporate sector. I was always looking and working toward the next promotion. I was always seeking out how I could earn my next raise. I was consumed with being the best. Why? Although I didn't know it then, I felt so much condemnation about who God created me to be that it propelled me to seek out validation in all the wrong areas of life.

I remember talking with my dad at age fifteen. I was just starting to look at what colleges I wanted to attend, what area of study I wanted to major in and I was *obsessed* with business. Like, completely, utterly, head over heels in love with business. When I told my dad what I wanted to do he paused. He said, "Well Gretchen, business is a tough world. Lots of competition and it's even tougher for females to make it. But, if that's what you want to do, just prepare yourself."

I looked at my dad, smirked and said, "Dad, I am going to have a big executive office with a black leather chair and nice, dark, cherry finished furniture with a candy dish on my desk." I said just like that with *that* much conviction. And although this chapter isn't geared toward power of the mind (we'll get there in a later chapter), you know what I left the very last day in my corporate career? An executive office with a black leather chair furnished with dark, cherry wood furniture…..AND in an industry that was considered a predominately *male driven industry*. So, if that's not getting specific with your vision, then I don't know what is. In fact, you know all those silly high school end-of-the-year things that go around and you can write down "where I will be in ten years?" I don't have mine any longer, but I even remember writing at age eighteen, I will be the CEO of an international business. Of course, I didn't do it in ten years. But, I sure did it in twelve.

But the condemnation I felt over those twelve years was immeasurable. I laid awake so many nights thinking, "What have I done, Lord?" I asked God all the time, "Why in the world did you hard wire me this way? Why can't I be a regular girl who just wants to be a stay-at-home mom, cook for her husband, raise my babies and do the 'mom' thing?" What's worse? I let *so* many people (both men and women) make me feel small or weird for wanting a successful career. Listen, ***female entrepreneurship is the new black.*** I just wasn't tuned into God's calling on my life. I had to go through a huge pile of crap to get to where I am at now. God had to restore my confidence in who I was in Him; not the world. I will 100% fully admit I was lost. I let the condemnation I felt be the driving force in guiding my spiritual compass in all the wrong directions; including my businesses.

Joyce Meyer brings up such a great point in her book, *Battlefield of the Mind.* I know I probably reference this book a lot, but it is so good, I can't not talk about it. In fact, when women come to me and start asking questions on "how do I start to fix 'X'," my first question is always "Have you read *Battlefield of the Mind* by Joyce Meyer?" Here is a little excerpt from her book that I had to share with you all. It really drives the point home of the confidence versus condemnation. Joyce refers to it as doubt and unbelief that steals our dreams in which God instills within us.

> *"God places dreams and visions in the hearts of His people; they begin as little 'seeds.' Just as a woman has a seed planted into her womb when she becomes 'pregnant,' so to speak, with the things God speaks and promises. During the 'pregnancy' Satan works hard to try and get us to 'abort' our dreams. One of the tools he uses is doubt; another is unbelief. Both of these work against the mind."*

Ever felt like that? Ever felt like, "Well, there is no use?" That is condemnation! There is no reason why you can't go and achieve your dreams. God didn't create you to be miserable. That is absurd. If you think I am excitable right now, you are absolutely correct. (You should see me when I speak in front of a group of women!) If we so much as give the enemy even a centimeter of room in our life, we risk our hopes and dreams being destroyed. John 10:10 (AMP) is on point with "the thief comes only in order to steal and kill and destroy. I came that they may have *and* enjoy life, and have it in abundance [to the full, till it overflows.]" Do you really think that God would have given you the dream and hope of a prosperous, thriving business all for nothing? No. I let the enemy condemn me for years, simply because I allowed the ridiculous notion that my dreams didn't matter and because they weren't what some in society would deem as "normal," therefore I turned to trying to earn my validation through the corporate realm, other modes of business and through empty performance metrics.

I get it. You are probably saying, "Yes. I am *so* there Gretchen, but have zero clue how to get out of it and move forward in my business and become a better leader." (Here is where you will need pen and paper because it's going to get real again.)

Fiercely You secret number three: You have the confidence within you, you just have to tap into it.

Here are three major differences between confidence and condemnation. I had to learn to teach myself these three in order to become the business woman I am today. (And no, not all at once.)

#1: Confidence says, "I can and I will." Condemnation says, "I can't, so I won't."

Let's go back to the network marketing world for a minute, since that is my area of expertise. Do you know how many people tell me, "Gretchen, I can't do what you do?" Countless. And my response is always the same. "Why not?" I am no different than the person next door to me. Age is nothing but a number, zip codes are nothing more than geographical territories, past backgrounds don't matter because they are in the past and the future isn't here yet. So why the heck can't you? You can. You're just telling yourself you can't. Condemnation is whispering, "Nope, you can't do that."

My favorite is when someone comes to me within my organization and says, "Well, I gave it thirty days and it didn't work, so I quit." That's like going to the gym for a month and trying to lose 100 pounds in 30 days and then when you don't lose the 100 pounds, you quit working out. It is a completely unrealistic goal. Is losing a 100 pounds a good goal to have? Absolutely! But let's set a realistic timeline. When people want to come into my organization, the first question I always ask is, "What are your expectations of success?" The reason I ask that is, I am up front, honest and real in that my business is not a get rich quick gig. You want to get rich quick (or die trying) go play the lottery. I don't have time for that. You *can* do it. You have to decide you *will* do it. Took me quite a while to get there myself, but I did it. Which brings me to number two.

#2: Confidence says, "I support them because _________." Condemnation says, "I am hating on them because _________."

Seriously, hating on people is just not cute. It's tasteless and furthermore, living in sin actually. My life coach, Cara Alwill Leyba, has a fantastic book out now called *Girl Code* and if you have not picked up the book, I highly recommend that you do. She has a chapter within the book entitled "The Power of Connection." There is a part within the chapter that specifically talks about *collaboration vs. competition* and it resonated so much with me. My absolute favorite part reads,

> *"Some of the best experiences of my career have involved collaboration. There is power in numbers, and women must realize that they do not have to ride this rollercoaster alone. Being an entrepreneur is isolation enough, so why separate yourself even more by competing with other women? Look around for people you can connect with and find ways to share, team up, and help each other out."*

To be specific in terms of network marketing (let's just stick with that example), I often hear "Well that person achieved 'X' in that amount of time. They didn't even work that hard." How do you know? They may be on their fourth pair of Louboutins because the first three pairs are all scuffed up from hitting the streets, rocking their business and getting back up again and moving forward. Condemnation is judging someone's story by the chapter you walked in on, and it's not cute; nor is it of God. You have to be confident. And let's be real, I wouldn't be writing any of this stuff and pouring my heart out if I hadn't gone through any of the same things you probably are experiencing right now reading this. I just had to, as one of my business partners says, learn how to "bless and release it." The only story you should be paying attention to is your own because if you aren't holding the pen when writing your story, someone else is. Be confident in who you are and have faith that God will complete the good work He started in you.

#3: Confidence says, "I have courage." Condemnation says, "I am scared because ________."

I will say from my own corporate experience that I had to have the courage to leave when the time came to leave. Was it scary? 1000%. But when I think back to where I was within the company, how much of my life was sucked away, how much time I missed with my children, how many hours of sleep I lost, how many times I woke up in the middle of the night with anxiety, how many Sunday nights I dreaded when the clock said 5:00pm and I thought about having to go back to work on Monday.....let me tell you how quickly my courage kicked it. And do I still struggle with it? Sure, who doesn't? I am human, just like you. But I have to make a daily, conscious effort to choose courage versus being scared and being ruled by fear. A lot of times, when I feel the fear creeping in again, I literally, out loud, ask myself, "Gretchen, what is your alternative?" When I think about what my alternative would be (staying in a job I hated and not living out my dreams and ambitions) girl.....did that change things quickly and jack up my confidence level!

Fear of Change is Subconscious

Did you know that most people fear change simply due to unconsciously believing that longevity somehow equals "good?" Here is what I mean by that. In a recent study, there were two groups of people at a college. The first group was told and educated that acupuncture had been in existence for over 2,000 years. The second group was told that acupuncture had only been around for 250 years. The first group expressed more interest and a favorable attitude toward acupuncture simply because it had been around longer (or so they thought). I truly believe that is why we view entrepreneurship (in a lot of situations) in a negative light. Sure, there is risk involved. There is also risk involved when you step into our car and drive down the street to your local Starbucks.

Here is another startling, but very real situation that I just came across a couple of weeks ago floating around social media. There was a status circulating around that read, "354 likes and 35 comments for a status post of 'I got a new job' and 8 likes and 2 comments for a status post of 'I started a small business'." Same principle applies. For some reason, we as a society have it engrained in our brains that we have to go to school and get a job to work 40 hours a week for 40 years to only have 40% of our retirement (if we are lucky) and somehow that receives praise. It receives praise because that has been the "longevity" for decades! I go places now, sometimes for coffee, sometimes to get my nails done, sometimes to the gym, sometimes to shop (just because I can in the middle of the day) and I look around at all the angry, unhappy, miserable, frustrated, sad and depressed people. It is all around us, just stop and take a look around. And inevitably my first thought is, "Why are they here even doing this? Why, if they are so miserable, are they continuing to come back day after day?" Truth is, partially they just flat out don't want to change and the other half of it is people really don't understand that there is another *real* way. They are stuck in the "longevity" of a J-O-B (or as I call it a "just over broke.").

I wasn't born to live this life in misery and neither were you. We weren't born to pay bills and then die. You have to take courage and catapult that unhappiness into action. This is by far one of my favorite verses in the Bible. I repeat it quite often, especially when I am feeling the enemy trying to creep in and stifle my business and call in life. The verse is Joshua 1:9 (AMP), "Have I not commanded you? Be strong and courageous! Do not be terrified or dismayed (intimidated), for the Lord your God is with you wherever you go." It took me a long time to really get that. And don't think that I still don't have to repeat this verse, like on the daily. The farther you go with your business and call in life, the *more* you have to repeat it. The more we have to cling to the promises God has already laid out for you and I. God doesn't care about our bank account, He cares about our faith account. And if you aren't making daily deposits, you'll inevitably end up overdrawing the account. You have to not only have confidence in what you are doing, but confidence in who you are in Jesus. Nothing else matters if you don't start there.

Another part of the world. An author, mother, leader and successful business woman

I want to introduce you to another fierce female I met solely via social media. She is an amazing women, a mom and bestselling author living in Bermuda (see how powerful social media is?) When I logged into one of her Periscopes for the first time, I was totally drawn in. She had *so* much life, she was absolutely gorgeous and I couldn't help but love her vibe. So naturally, being the crazy person I am in networking, I totally reached out to her and said, "I have to feature you in the book." Her name is Gaynetė Edwards. She is the bestselling author of *Lucky Code*, has been featured in Huffington Post *and* Success (which by the way are two of my most favorite business publications to read) and she lives in Bermuda. So excited to bring her to you.

Social Media

Instagram: @gaynete
Periscope: @gaynete
Twitter: @gaynete

So tell us about you!

I am a mom, model and former Miss Teen Bermuda Islands and a UN Youth Leader. I am also a bestselling author and a contributor for Huffington Post.

When did you realize you were an entrepreneur?
From a very young age I had an entrepreneurial spirit. I used to cut my dad's old clothes to make outfits for Barbies and sell them on the side of the street. I also collected golf balls near courses and sold them. It was something invigorating about being able to fulfill a need and generate income without someone giving me instructions. I loved that.

As a mom and a business woman, how do you balance everything?
I've realized that I work best super early in the morning. Because of this, I get up early and sort out everything I have to do and tackle the biggest tasks first. I also prioritize pretty well. Family comes first so if it's a matter of choosing between an honor roll assembly at school for my daughter and a business task, the assembly will win every time.

How do you see yourself the way Jesus sees you?
I try not to take life too seriously and laugh at my mistakes when I can. Perfection is never my goal. It's simply to improve daily, helping as many as I can along the way.

Do you have a mission statement/vision statement and if so what is that? How did you arrive at that mission/vision statement?
My mission statement is constantly evolving as I do. I tend to live by quotes and have so many favorites. One that immediately comes to mind is by Winston Churchill, "You'll never reach your destination if you stop to throw stones at every dog that barks."

What inspires you the most in your entrepreneurial journey?
I try to find inspiration in everything around me. Success stories and getting positive feedback from those in my community makes my heart beam. Being in a position to be a positive example for my little girl is another highlight.

What fears do you have and how have you (or do you) overcome them?
I have many fears and push through them daily. I understand that I have to feel my fear and do the exact thing that terrifies me in order to succeed. An example of this is when I was terrified of sharing my message over video but knew that I could reach a much larger audience doing this. I committed to doing frequent YouTube videos and Periscopes to assist me to get over the fear. Only when you face your fears head on, do you step into your power.

What advice do you have for women who struggle with finding and/or holding on to their determined why?
I don't think anyone can force your why or will upon you. It's something we must find for ourselves.

What is the number one thing you have learned in your journey as a Jesus girl in business?
You can't worry about what others are saying or doing. Stay focused on your truth and keep it moving.

What is one thing you do every single day?
Give. Even if just a smile or a genuine compliment. Giving is something each of us can do daily.

How do you stay disciplined in your business?
I keep the end in view. Knowing where I want to be and all the lives I want to touch keeps me motivated to continue on.

So, know that as a female entrepreneur, we all come in contact with some sort of feelings of fear and condemnation. But the beauty part is, we don't have to accept that as our truth. We are who we are, perfectly created in the image of Christ. Don't ever let anyone in this world make you feel that what you are doing is crazy or isn't worth it. Believe me, it is worth it. Listening to that still small voice in your hear and in your soul, is 100% absolutely worth it. Every minute of it.

Coffee Thoughts:

1. What is one thought of condemnation you are going to let go of today and give over to God?

____

2. What is one fear you are going to let go of in your life and/or business?

____

3. What are you going to start saying "I can and I will" to and what are you going to stop saying "I can't so I won't" to?

____

CHAPTER 4

WHEN IN DOUBT, WRITE IT OUT

"I speak best when I write."

–Gretchen Barocio

Just write it down

Yes, you guessed it. I speak the best when I write. And when in doubt, I always write it out. Whether it is my business plan, my ideas, the next blog I am going to write, or the next workshop I am going to conduct, whatever it is.....I always write it down. I can't even count how many times I have ripped myself from a deep sleep in the middle of the night in some frantic panic to find my phone because some crazy idea popped into my head that I have to record. I think that is why entrepreneurs have a hard time getting started sometimes. They don't write it out, they just simply start something without a plan. And I am not even talking about having the most detailed, well thought out, massively organized plan. I am simply talking about just writing *anything* down that comes to mind.

I love Mark Twain's spin on writing, "Writing is easy. All you have to do is cross out the wrong words." Meaning, just get something down and from there, add, delete or change whatever you need to change. My content is always evolving because as I write more ideas down, additional content always comes up. You have to think of writing it out, even if it just a few words, like you would finding that perfect pair of shoes or outfit. What do you do when you are shopping for the perfect outfit or that perfect pair of shoes? You start collecting pictures, adding it to your Pinterest boards, shopping around, trying them on and then, once you've found that perfect outfit or that perfect pair of Louboutins, you just know it! It hits your gut and gives you goosebumps. But you aren't going to get the right pair of shoes, the right business model or the right brand if you don't start somewhere.

The power of images. The power of words.

Here is something else that happens when you write it out. I am sure most of you reading this have done some sort of dream boarding session, whether that was for your yearly goals, your business goals, your life goals, etc. When you take those dreams, those visions, those goals and put that pen to paper it is unbelievable the shift that happens with your mindset. I am going to tell you all little story just how powerful that was in my life.

As most of you know, I had the privilege of working with Cara Alwill Leyba having her as my Master Life Coach. One of the most basic, yet most empowering exercises she had me do in one of our one on one sessions was writing out my resignation letter. At the time, I was still in working in the corporate jail, really not enjoying my job at all and honestly and I was so borderline depressed that I couldn't work on my businesses full time because of my day job. (Believe me, I know about having a day job and working your side hustle. It ain't easy.) I daily envisioned walking into my boss' office and giving my two week notice. I am not joking when I say I would literally envision it. I would play it over and over in my mind what I was going say, how I was going to make my exit, how I wanted to leave for good, how I would drive out of the parking lot, even down to what song I would be blasting out my car window upon leaving.

In the one on one session, Cara asked me, "Why don't you write out your resignation letter? Don't send it necessarily but write it down and get it out on paper." I was like *ummm duh, lightbulb.* Why had I not done that before? Why had I not done the very thing I've done with all my other ideas and business plans? What would be any different about writing out my resignation letter? So I did. Once I had written it out, I emailed it off to Cara that Sunday night. Now of course she was in New York, so I knew she wouldn't receive it until the next morning. Monday morning rolls around, I woke up to her response and she wrote back, "CHILLS. If you don't send it to them [the company] it needs to be in the book." So before I let you in on my resignation letter, let me fill you in on what quickly happened after that. And by quickly, I mean within *hours.*

That same morning at about nine in the morning, my regional vice president called me into his office, sat me down and had the most distraught look on his face. He said, "it pains me to have to do this, nor did I want to spend my Monday morning before Thanksgiving having have this conversation but the company is eliminating your position. I have, in writing here, your options. One of which, you can take position 'x'' for $5,000 less a year or option two, take a four month severance package."

Can you imagine my astonishment when hours before (not even twelve hours before to be exact) I wrote out my resignation letter? I was being given not only the opportunity to leave with my integrity intact and my dignity at an all-time high, I was going to be compensated for it. (And yes, I called Cara like *immediately* upon leaving my VP's office and was jumping and dancing all over my office.) I obviously don't need to tell you what option I took. Fast forward to today, and I've never gone back to having a boss other than myself since. And it has been the absolute *best* decision of my business career.

My point? When in doubt (or fear, frustration, uncertainty) write it out! There is pure magic that happens when you put that pen to paper with what you truly want to accomplish. So as promised, here is the letter I wrote to my CEO (and of course, I changed the names to protect integrity.)

Re: Resignation for Gretchen Barocio, employee: Profit Center 123

ATTEN: Office of the President

Mr. Boss,

My name is Gretchen Barocio. I was one of your Corporate Executives at Profit Center 123 and have been with ABC for a little over seven years. It both pains and releases me to write this to you. I would be doing a huge disservice to both myself and fellow executives if I did not tell you the real reasons behind my resignation. By the time you read this, I will be long gone so you won't need to worry about firing me nor will need to worry about the need to protect ABC's reputation. I am not here to speak ill will about ABC; however, know that what I have to say is what those of us middle executives all feel and want to say; but don't have the executive balls to say.....so let me say it for them.

The corporate America structure is the worst I have ever seen it. Not only is it a derailment of American family life, which is what our country was once built on, it is the epitome of self-destruction and self-doubt. The best thing ABC did for me was help me understand what was really important. And I will tell you it isn't the bottom line. It's the fact that there are many who are already at their rock bottom in life, some who inevitably work for you, and instead of finding refuge and worth in their role within ABC, they are treated like a commodity and a number on the page. Shame on me for thinking I could ever change that. I have spent years learning from the best of the best leaders in the industry of leadership including Jeff Olson, John Maxwell and Howard Shultz. I have beat my head against every wall within the confines of the 123's building only to realize there isn't anything that I really am "free" to do as a leader. I've heard "a good leader can turn around any profit center" but what you fail to realize is that you've lost most of them at this point. And sadly, the ones that are still around are sacrificing their family time, their integrity (in some senses) and their overall quality of life to bring a freaking dollar to the bottom line for people they will never meet.

Here is what I know. I know you don't sleep at night. I know you probably lay awake and either toil over the pressure upon you or take some sort of medication to help you sleep (in hopes it keeps you soundly asleep) until you have to wake up and live the nightmare all over again. And if you are sleeping soundly at night, without anything to aid the stress, then shame on you. I don't know how you could in good conscience. I have spent the last seven years at the beck and call of all the things I said I would never do. I never thought I would end up in such a dishonest trade.

Second, there is no way you pay your people enough for the amount of time and servanthood they provide to this organization. People like me are one in a million and it's a shame you lost me. ABC says they "value" their people but I'd love to see how that really looks, as I have yet to see it. I spent over two months putting back together a sinking ship. I lost time with my husband, my children, my health took a huge back seat and I almost ended up in the hospital with a horrible bronchial infection. But again, who up at the top would care about that? We are made to feel that any small success is worthless, that it doesn't matter and that "well, that's what you get a paycheck for." If I had to put a monetary value on my people here, I would say they are invaluable. There isn't any amount of money that would cover what they have done for the public.

Third, I love it when people talk about "pyramid" schemes. I love it because I laugh and I want to scream at the top of my lungs, "Listen all you corporate America people, you ARE in the epitome of a pyramid scheme." The whole corporate America structure is a dang pyramid. You have one person (or maybe a few) that make all the money while the rest of us slave away and those at the top place their "worth" on us based on the amount we are paid. It's capped out at a ceiling rate. I will tell you this, you have truly made me realize that I am worthy of what I deem to be paid and I will never let anyone else place that worth on me but Jesus and I. I am worth far more than what ABC pays me bi-monthly and certainly worth far more than how ABC treats me. And then on top of that, I am told when and when I am not able to take vacation? It's much less than a corporate America "business" structure, it seems more little like prison to me. Correct me if I am wrong.

Fourth, you will lose more people. Why? Because this is the age of the 'ENTREPRENEUR.' The best thing that ABC did for me was help me understand that I was in a trap and that entrepreneurship was my way to get out. And not only get out, but have the best laid plan in place that trumps anything that any corporate organization could lay out for me. I remember the national conference call about two years ago, going over and breaking down the new employee bonus program and I remember laughing thinking, "Are they really serious? Is this a joke?" And I remember it came up on the call that someone said, "You have so much potential to make A LOT of money." Let's be crystal clear. A lot of money means NO CAP. Endless.....not what ABC deems. But, hey, I get it. There has to be enough for the greedy at the top. Don't want to disappoint the shareholders and their quiet evening at home sipping wine and eating dinner with their family while the rest of us slave away missing dinner with ours.

Fifth, we are made to feel shame for WHO we are as people. We can't be ourselves due to the insurmountable cloud of political bureaucracy looming over the entire corporate America world. Tell me how THAT makes an enjoyable work environment? Oh wait, it doesn't. I am tired of hiding behind who I really am and was created to be. As well, I am disappointed that I sought to get the approval through corporate America versus what and where I know my true value lies. I am disappointed I let it go on for as long as I did. But, I will say this, I am darn proud that I made the choice I did and am on my way to where I know, without a shadow of doubt, I should be going. And the beauty part of it is, while you are reading this, there isn't anything you can do to stop me because I am already gone and going to where I know I am destined to be.

Sixth, my hope and prayer is that this letter, once released, will help others realize that it's not about ABC specifically that wrecks someone's self-worth, fosters self-doubt and self- disqualification, but that it is solely due to the fact that we aren't able to be who God created us to be in such a restrictive environment as Corporate America in general. We aren't able to be the very thing any company needs because we are told what we are supposed say, what we are supposed to do and how we are supposed to do it. There is a "script" for everything. I will say this, Jesus and I will write the script and story from now on. Never again, will I let someone else do it for me.

Make no mistake.....I am not ungrateful for the seven-plus years that ABC had in my life. If anything, it has re-birthed and ignited who I really am, what is truly important and what is the ultimate call on my life. I weep for those who are still stuck in the trap of corporate America and a job they hate. But make no mistake about this, I WILL sleep soundly at night knowing who I am, where I am rooted and where I am going and helping others that are where I used to be.

With that, I, Gretchen Barocio, officially resign with ZERO intention to ever come back. And honestly, whether you do anything with this or not, is of no value to me. You just need to know and I needed to be the voice for those who feel they don't have one. So know you know. Sleep well, I know I will.

Sincerely,

Gretchen Barocio, former executive for Profit Center 123 and Creator and Founder of TheGirlpreneur.com

Fiercely You secret number four: Pen to paper is magic. If you have anything that is looming inside, anything that could potentially be tearing you apart, I urge you to put it down on paper. We cannot grow as Jesus would intend us to do harboring resentment and bitterness. Harboring anger and resentment is not of Jesus either. We can't get to where we are going without a plan either. It doesn't have to be a perfect plan, only God's plan is perfect. But we have to be open to hear it, open to receive it and willing to let go of the things we cannot control.

Team #Bossbabe extraordinaire, YouTube expert and mom.

So this girl is also super special to me. I have so very much enjoyed working with her in both the #Bossbabe realm and on this project. Jessika and I met virtually last year during a Periscope I caught on the #TeamBossbabe channel. Her energy was infectious, so I did what I naturally do and I Instagram researched her. When I saw she was also a Jesus girl, I had to talk to her. I reached out to her via direct message, we started chatting and I just knew in my heart I had to include her in this project. She is an amazing millennial, a network marketer, one of the five core girls on #TeamBossbabe and a Jesus girl full of determination and life. I would kick it with this girl in Louboutins any day of the week. Sit tight and get into your "boss mode" to read this girl's story.

Social Media
Periscope: @Jessika_fancy
Instagram: @Jessika_Fancy
Twitter: @Jessika_fancy
YouTube: **youtube.com/jessikafancy**

So tell us about yourself!
Well, okay. Ummmm, I am a mom, a student and teacher all the same time. I believe that we are never too old to learn. I come from a military background, I have traveled a lot, lived over seas, experienced different types of cultures and am also a college graduate. Sometimes I feel like because I am not even using my degree, that it was kind of a waste of time. I felt like I went to college because that is what we were *supposed* to do. My family is from the Caribbean. My parents wanted me to get an education and I wanted to make them proud. Now I am not using my degree because I am not passionate about it. I majored in hospitality and hotel management. I went to the number two school in the nation for that particular field, but I am not just passionate about it. I attended University of Central Florida and when I finished, I just knew I really wanted to work for myself. I've always hustled.

Nowadays, we don't have go to college, get married right away and have kids. We have so many choices and we should really focus on doing what we are passionate about and what makes us happy.

When did you realize you were you were an entrepreneur?
I first realized when I was in high school. My parents divorced when I was only two years old, so I had a step mom and a step dad. My step dad is a hustler. My step parents never treated me like a step child. I always watched my step dad in his hustle and it just inspired me! I wanted to do that because I knew I had talents and gifts. Then in college I started my YouTube channel and then that is when I realized I wanted to do something on the side. It also inspired and helped me not be afraid of hustling when I created my YouTube channel. I have so much fun with it. I was not afraid of network marketing. Once you have that entrepreneurial mentality, you just start to not care what people think. It's as if it has been engrained for years within me.

As a young mom, how do you balance life, motherhood and business?
I am still trying to find that balance. My baby is only one. And with every single person you have to be the judge for you. Everyone is different. You have to decide when your baby is napping, do I nap? Or do I work on my business? Or do I work on something else? It's different being a mom because along with being a business owner you have to cook, clean, run a business and all the other stuff that just comes along with normal life, but it is possible. It just takes time to work through what works best for you. Like I said in my Periscope earlier today, "don't be afraid to ask for help." Don't be ashamed of that. It's all about each individual finding out what works for them.

How do you see yourself as Jesus sees you?
A work in progress. It's okay to realize and accept that no one is perfect. God isn't asking us to be perfect. He doesn't want us to know all the answers either. It's not on us to have it all figured out. I have always known I was different. I never knew what it was. I feel like I am such a......I don't know how to explain it. I have two different sides to me. I like being in front of the camera, I like to go first, but at the same time I am introvert and shy. I have always struggled with "why am I outgoing and why I am I shy?" I stopped trying to be someone else. Jesus just loves me the way I am. I wanted to be a "BA" when I was younger, I thought that was cool. I wanted to be strong and assertive, but now I just want to be nice, I like being kind to people and we need more of that in the world. I have no problem being kind now. It's fun! Not that I wanted to mean to begin with, but I just wanted to be strong and assertive. But you can be strong, assertive and kind all at the same time. I think we all struggle with stuff inside of us. I embrace both. I am such a contradiction and I love that. It gives me layers. I can be a public speaker, but at the same time I can say "I don't want to go out and be social."

Do you have a mission statement, and if so, what is it? How did you come up with it?
You know? I don't really have one. I want to figure one out. The think what comes to me when I think vision or mission statement is "find your passion and execute it the best way possible for you." I feel like people need to figure out what makes them happy and figure out the best way to

accomplish it. We cannot make other people happy, especially if we are not happy on the inside with who we are.

What inspires you the most in your entrepreneurial journey?

Honestly.....it's so I can take care of my family. My family is not from this country. I grew up with not a lot of money, and we weren't poor by any means, but I come from a blended family. When I was younger I always wanted to help people. I remember distinctly when I was younger I always wanted to help people and I was like "God why do I want to help people before myself?" I want to put it all on my back and take care of other people for those that have carried everything on their back for me for so long.

What fears do you have and how have you (or do you) overcome them?

A big fear of mine was disappointing my parents. I was afraid of disappointing my dad. Now that I have decided that YouTube and my business is what I really want to do, that is what I am going to. I am not afraid of my decision. Overcoming that is just being sure in your decision. Have a conversation with the person (or people) that don't understand and explain your point of view. If they love you and are on board with you, great! And if not, then be okay with it. God didn't intend for you to fit in. I don't want to have a 9-5 job. This is what I am going to make a career of. Don't be afraid of what they are going to say. Ask yourself, "Do I want to a job that I hate every day?" Today there is no limit on what we can do.

What advice do you have for women who struggle with finding and holding onto their determined why?
Don't have a fantasy in your head of what you think entrepreneurship is like. It's hard work, it's a commitment, it's work. You can't start a project or a business and think that it's going to go just as planned. It's going to be a rollercoaster. You need to make that your mindset before you even start. It's going to be harder before it gets easier. It takes on to five years to grow your business and become confident in what you are doing. It's not going to go the way you think. If you are reading this book and want to be an entrepreneur, understand that it's not going to be easy, but *it is going to worth it.* It will be worth the blood, sweat, tears and prayers to see it evolve the way it will evolve.

What is the number one thing you have learned in you journey as a Jesus girl and as business woman?
The number one thing I've learned is do not be afraid to bring anything to Him. I talk to Him all the time about everything in my business. I talk to Him about bringing me the best of the best. If I am going through something, I will ask Him for the things I want and need to work on. Don't be afraid to talk to Him; whether out loud or to yourself. It might feel weird talking out loud but, it is so good and so empowering. I am not afraid to talk to Him out loud anymore. Especially when I am in a spot of telling Him "I need your help to be better at 'x'." Ask and you shall receive, but if you ask not, you have not.

What is one thing you do every single day?
I express gratitude. I am always expressing gratitude. Whether it be a clean carpet, my toilet, my shower, my bed to sleep in. Every day before I go to bed, I say all the things I am grateful for. The hair on my head. I try not to talk negatively about anything. I try not to even think about it. I express gratitude on the little things. I express gratitude when things are going wrong too, not just when they are going right. Express to Him the gratitude for all the little things. Sense of smell, internet, clothes on your back, the socks on your feet, all the little things that some people in this world may not have.

How do you stay disciplined in your business?
Oh man, that's a great question. I think that is something that people have to learn how to do. I reason with myself and understand that what I am doing now will pay

dividends in the future. I understand that if I give up that hour of sleep to get the work done now, it feels better later. To harvest, you have to sow seeds. It's all in your mind. Discipline is mind game. You have to make up your mind to stay disciplined.

So ladies, we have the power within us. We just need to throw it out there and really use it.

Coffee Thoughts:

1. What is one thing you need to write down right now? A business plan? Your deepest struggle? (I urge you to share that with someone you value and trust. No road should be traveled alone.)

____

____

____

____

____

2. Once your business plan, struggle, etc is written down and shared, what is the timeline you are going to put on it? Make a deadline for taking action on either starting the business, or addressing the root of what is holding you back.

____

____

____

____

____

CHAPTER 5

HAVE A BACKBONE, NOT A WISHBONE

"Stop wearing your wishbone where your backbone ought to be."

–Unknown

Digging deep for that strength

One of the things you have to master as an entrepreneur is strengthening that backbone. And I am not talking physically, although I am a huge believer in living a healthy lifestyle through fitness and good eating habits. I am talking about when you are going out there and putting your hopes, wishes and dreams on the line and really going for it, be prepared to meet opposition. It's going to happen. I have lost many friends over my entrepreneurial lifetime. And in the beginning, I am also not going to lie and say it was fun and enjoyable. It's really not. In fact, I lost my best friend of twenty-four years going after my dreams. Was it enjoyable? Totally not, but in the end I still came out on the other side. Relationships, whether with significant others, family members or friends are always tough when there is a "break-up" involved.

Building a foundation

I am a huge believer in prayer being the foundation in which you build your backbone. There is no way I would have been able to get through losing a friend of twenty-four years, among many other things, without massive amounts of prayer in my life. Knowing that everything I do starts and ends with God, and that prayer is always my first line of defense in making sure my backbone is strong. If it's all done via my own efforts, I will inevitably miss the mark. Now don't get me wrong, you must put in a decent amount of effort when building a business or a brand. God isn't going to do for you what He knows you can do for yourself, but He will most certainly partner with you and fill in the gap where you can't with your own efforts. It has to start with your backbone, how well you maintain that backbone and how well you continue to build that backbone.

One of my most favorite women in the Bible is Sarah, Abraham's wife. Let me breakdown Sarah's story real quick (and yes I will keep it very modern so it's easy to understand). Sarah married Abraham, who was declared as the "father of many nations." See in my business mind, I picture Abraham being dubbed the Bill Gates or Jeff Olson of the business world before it even happens, as in Abraham is going to straight dominate. Abraham was assured he was going to have a son. Months, years and decades passed without any sign of a son being born. In fact, Sarah not only ended up barren, she ended up barren in a society where a woman's measure of worth was based on her ability to bear children. How embarrassing right? God promises them a child, the married couple whose husband is supposed to be the "father of many nations" and then ends up childless? By the time Sarah reaches age ninety, she is on the brink of pretty much giving up. And to be quite honest, if it were me, I would have given up hope by age 35 (just being real).

On the other hand though, Abraham held on to God's promise of bearing him a son. He never let go of it. He never lost sight of it, even when his own wife was in disbelief. Long story short, they ended up having a son, whom they named Isaac when Sarah was ninety years old. Talk about nothing being impossible. What I love about this story and what it exemplifies is the life lesson of when we are swimming in self-doubt, dissatisfaction of our situation(s) or compelled by fear, we just have to ask ourselves, "Is anything too hard for God?"

There isn't anything too hard for God nor is there any limit to what He can do. So what do you do when you are refining that backbone, when you are in the trenches of feeling like your business isn't going the way you want it to or things aren't falling into place? Aside from prayer, I am going to breakdown three mini points that literally catapulted my network marketing business and brand once I put them into practice.

Fiercely You Fire Starters: 3 ways to ignite your business and build your backbone:

#1: Assess or Reassess your Inner Circle.
I cannot say enough how important this business strategy is. A great tip I picked up on one of my network marketing calls when I first started in the business (and it has stuck with me ever since) is: pull out your phone and look at the last five text messages, read them and who they are from. That will tell you all you need to know about your inner circle.

Now by the time this book is fully published, my list may look at little different, but I will use myself as an example, right here and now. The last five text messages and who they are from below are:

First one: (Erin Nicole, one of my business partners) "No it's a meeting to learn about what we do for our businesses so we can help him load the information into the business community group and get referrals for each other."

Second one: (Lisa R, one of my best friends in the whole wide world) "Not even going to lie, this made my day" (me referring to a message I had received.)

Third one: (Ver Kelly- whom you met and read about earlier in this book) "Totally agree. Do it!!!" (In reference to an opportunity that was presented to me.)

Fourth one: (Josh Gonzales- my graphic designer for this book): "Shoot, totally forgot to send the information with Aaron this morning. Are you going to be at the church tomorrow?"

Fifth one: (Aaron Barocio- my husband) "Call me when you are on your way home" (which of course I called him.)

And for good measure, I will just throw in a sixth one: (From my network marketing home business office in Addison, Texas): "Stay up to date today with the latest information coming from headquarters."

My point to that little exercise? My inner circle is in support of me, they are part of my backbone. I will not allow people into my life or my inner circle that tear me down, dump on my positive vibes or ruin my business and most importantly, interfere with my relationship with Jesus. And as harsh as this may sound, one of my other business partners said to me once, "Gretchen, people are either in the way or on the way with you." I never forgot that.

#2: Do it afraid.
This tip is straight from the beautiful Domonique Price, whom you will read about later in this book. This refers to taking your comfort zones and throwing them out the window. When you are running a business, which is hard in itself, the last thing you need paralyzing you is your fear. So just do it afraid. Domonique is a perfect example of living that out. You will get to read her story later about how she overcame some major hurdles and fears: everything from going through pageant competitions, to being crowned Miss Oregon 2015 in the Miss USA pageant, to becoming the youngest attorney in the Portland Trailblazers' history. My point? We are human. There will be fears, but what lies on the other side of that fear is something phenomenal. So do it afraid if you have to, but do it.

#3: If you are the smartest person in the room, time to pick up your heels and coffee and move to another room.
What do I mean by that? Personal development is key. You cannot *ever* stop being a student; especially when it comes to your business. I have stories beyond stories where continuing my journey as a student has paid off in more ways than just financially. You cannot stop learning about your passion or your craft. Not only to ensure that you are staying up on the "latest and greatest" but more importantly, to become the best version of you. I am convinced God did not put me on this earth to waste time. I am here to make a difference and change lives.

Of course, changing habits can be tough. I will be the first to admit that I used to watch a lot of TV to fill my vacant time. I would pour a glass of wine after a long day (yes,

Jesus girls have a glass of wine every now and again) and turn on the TV to see nothing but crappy news and horrible reality TV shows. My TV watching days just ended with my mind to becoming filled with garbage. And as the old saying goes, it truly is "garbage in, garbage out." So make sure you are taking time to evaluate what you are filling your time with. Are the things you are doing high payoff activities or are they "time suckers?" Are you the smartest person in the room? If so, pick those Louboutins up and starts hustling to the next room, girl.

Fiercely You secret number five: Seize opportunity when it presents itself. Chances are it will never come around again.

One of my business partners says to me all the time when I am teetering between seizing opportunity or letting it pass my by is, "Gretchen, stop 'getting ready' to get ready." What she means by that is, stop waiting until you are 100% ready to make the change. Let's be real about something. You are never going to be 100% ready. That's like someone saying, "We aren't going to have children until we are financially ready." As a parent myself, unless you are Bill Gates, you'll never be financially ready. There is no manual that comes with being a parent either. You just step into that role when it happens and figure it out as you go. The same is true when it comes to entrepreneurship and *especially* as a mom I might add. But honestly, it can be applied to anyone at any age.

It's the whole "if/then" statement. *If I had a million dollars, then I'd start my business.* Who says you have to have a million dollars to start a business? I only had $500 and I parlayed that into an international network marketing business, a brand and now a book. When there is a will, there is a way. I am not saying make unwise financial decisions. Not in the slightest, but any and every female entrepreneur I work with, collaborate with, commune with, network with….. all say the same thing. You'll never be fully ready, you just have to take action at some point. Because if you don't, you'll end up wasting thirty years getting ready to get ready to make a change, and before you know it, life will have passed you by.

Don't ignore God's purpose for your life.

I truly believe God has a purpose for each and every one of us. I truly believe He created you for something wonderful. Something amazing and powerful. But if you ignore the call on your life, if you ignore that still small voice that resides inside of you, if you aren't going to follow the call God has for you, He'll find someone else to do it for Him. He will find someone else willing and up for the call. And it won't matter if that person is "equipped" for it or not; He'll equip them anyway. He's God. He's capable of anything. I ignored the call on my life for years until I woke up and really paid attention. Once I did that, I can't even begin to tell you the doors that opened. Even now sitting here writing this out, I am still astonished that some things are happening simply because I said, "Yes, Lord. I will go there. I will do this because You are asking me to."

I finally reached a point in my life that I made a promise to God that I would never ignore the call again. I told Him I would never hold back on the opportunities He has for me and that I will always step out in faith, even if it means no one believes it will happen but He and I. And I've been there too. Sometimes you may be the only one who sees it, but that is where faith has to step in. That is where God steps in and does the very things we can't do on our own. And as an entrepreneur and business owner, I need that. You need God to step in and fill the gaps in your business because you can't fill them in on your own. So when the phone of opportunity rings, answer it.

The Queen of Social Media

So in that spirit, I'd like to introduce the next fierce female I want to share with you. Someone who, when I first started to launch my brand via Periscope, I was glued, I mean *glued* to this woman's teachings. She taught me so much in the social media realm, so much about business and entrepreneurship and, honestly, when I first began to write this book, I was incredibly scared to even reach out to her and ask for an interview. In fact, I wasn't confident that she'd even respond to my message that I had sent because I knew how busy she was. So, of course, I was floored and astonished when she did write me back and said, "Absolutely! I'd love to be a part of the project." I about died. Not going to lie.

Kim Garst, Founder and CEO of Boom! Social, is a personal branding and social media business consultant. It is what her firm does completely. She is a bestselling author, she has been a keynote speaker (several times) and is the *First Lady of Periscope.* She has done in-depth trainings for both entrepreneurs as well as Corporations (such as IBM). She has appeared in Digital Journal and BIB podcasts.

She is ranked in the top 50 list of social media influencers in Forbes, recognized by startupnations.com as one of Top 200 Leading Moms in Business and one of the Top 100 Branding Experts to follow on Twitter. She is someone who has influenced me greatly in my journey, my brand and is so down to earth. She is a Jesus girl too, and not afraid to let people know. So, as promised, here is the juicy interview with Kim Garst.

Social Media
Instagram: @kimgarst
Twitter: @kimgarst
Periscope: @kimgarst
Facebook: Kim Garst (fan page)

So tell us about you!
I love God, family and hockey. I am a social media guru helping small business owners unlock the keys to social media selling! I am an author, keynote speaker and the first lady of Periscope. I have been working in the social media and online realm for almost 25 years.

When did you realize you were an entrepreneur?
I don't know that I ever really realized it. When I first started out it was to make an extra $200 for the car payment each month. And from there it just sort of evolved. I tell a lot of people that I am an "accidental entrepreneur." (laughing) I don't think I ever really woke up one day and said, "Today I am going to be an entrepreneur." It just happened over time.

Starting out, how did you balance it all? Mom, children, business, etc?

Wow, it was hard. When I started almost twenty-five years ago..... you just had to do what you had to do. I can remember being on the floor playing with Legos in one hand and the phone in the other. I remember my kids saying, "No more phone, Mom." I always say to entrepreneurs, women in particular, "be present where you are." I think that is my only one regret. I thought I was doing what I needed to do. I just wished I spent a little more time being present where I needed to be at the time I was in during those moments.

How do you see yourself as Jesus sees you?

I hope that He sees me as someone who doesn't leave Him at the door. I used to be so scared mixing my faith and business, but now it really is just a part of who I am. I don't try to hide who I am. He has to be first in everything I do.

Do you have a mission/vision statement and if so, what is it?

It's funny you ask that because I was just on the phone with my business partner talking about this very exact thing! We were discussing the re-vamping of our mission statement, finalizing some things.....but honestly it has always been about service and making a difference. We want to always take what we know and pass that information along. If I can curve the learning curve for people, I want to be able to do that.

What inspires you the most in your entrepreneurial journey?

Oh, making a difference in people's lives and service absolutely. After being in business for almost twenty-five years now, I never forget where I came from. It took me five years to earn my first $60. Not kidding! We just didn't have the resources back then that we do today. Today it's like we almost have too many to choose from. It was a struggle back then for the resources and now, today, it's a struggle to know what to choose from to use. So I work to shorten that learning curve for as many people as possible.

What fears do you have and how do you overcome them?

Anytime I feel fear I cuddle up to it and make it my "BFF" and face it head on. You really can't let it control you. I always say that if you are meeting resilience or feeling resistance, you know you are on the right path. My goal this year, though, in terms of fear, is starting to defy more of those other fears like my fear of heights (laughing). But in terms of my business, I know that when I meet resistance I am certainly on the right path.

What advice do you have for women out there who may be struggling to hang on to that WHY?

Oddly enough, most people don't define their WHY right away when they start. Most people start the journey and make it all about the money. And making money is okay, but it can't be the only reason you are doing what you are doing. At the root, our businesses can't be about us. It has to be about service to someone (or the masses depending on your type of business). If you are in service to someone else, the money will appear. Take that passion of yours (whatever it is) and figure out a way to turn that into a service.

What is the number one thing you have learned as a Jesus girl and business woman?

Don't worry about what other people think. I used to worry about what people would think about me and what I stood for in terms of my beliefs, business and my faith together. And I have a lot of clients that don't have the same belief system I do and that is totally okay. I am okay with that, but that doesn't mean I hide from who I am and what I believe. I just got to a point where I am okay to attract what I put out there. There are a lot of clients I have that are in alignment with my beliefs as well. But you generally attract what you believe. It's the law of attraction.

What is one thing you do every single day?

I read my Bible and pray. It's interesting because I see a lot of people and interact with a lot of clients and sometimes when they are talking to me and quoting something in terms of a business practice, they don't realize that it is actually derived from the Word. There are basic business principles that are rooted in the Bible. In fact, I am debating whether or not I want to do a Periscope about this, well not necessarily *this*, but about influencers bashing influencers on social media. The Bible is very specific in that if you have an issue with someone or a problem....you go directly to that person right? Don't throw it out there on Facebook, email, text, etc.....face it.

How do you stay disciplined in your business?
I pray every day and read my Bible. It has to happen daily otherwise the rest just doesn't fall into place.

So ladies, grab a cup of coffee and curl up with some time to digest what you just read.

Coffee Thoughts:

1. What is one thing you are going to do this week to change your wishbone into a backbone?

____

____

____

____

____

2. What are you going to bring to God in order for Him to be able to start working and change you and your business?

____

____

____

____

____

CHAPTER 6

SOMETIMES YOU HAVE TO WEAR THE CROWN AND HEELS, EVEN IF YOU DON'T FEEL LIKE IT.

"If you are going through hell, keep going."

–Winston Churchill

Perseverance versus hard work

I tell you what, perseverance is the hard work you end up having to do when you get tired of the hard work you already did. And it can feel like hell. Even in the midst of writing this book, there have been nights where I was balling so hard and the mascara had clouded my vision so much, that I had to stop and breathe and just remember.... this, too, shall pass. See, I am a huge dreamer, I am doer, I am mover and a shaker. And that scares people, sometimes myself included. But as I have stated before in this book, nothing good comes from our comfort zones. When I finally quit my corporate job, there was a whole different approach to entrepreneurship I had to take. My hard work and determination took a violent shove into perseverance. I had to get up earlier, sometimes stay up later, do research, re-do, re-write, re-vamp, re-calculate, etc. When being an entrepreneur, you have to get used to the "RE" in re-do.

Here is where I am going to get tough. You cannot allow yourself to slip into the mindset that just because something didn't work out well the first time around, that it automatically means it's time to give up. You need to give up on giving up. I actually just bought a workout T-shirt that says that. And I love it because it really is a truth bomb. The actual *Siri* definition of persevere is to "continue in a course of action even in the face of difficulty or with little or no prospect of success." So, give up on giving up. Before I get into my next interview, which I am super excited to share in this chapter, I want to share a little excerpt from a blog post I published in early January of this year (so, yes, this is very fresh and recent.) It was actually at a point when the book was coming to an end and I was working to wrap up interviews with people and securing times to chat with each fierce female, things just kind of felt (notice how I said "felt") out of control. I felt so down. People were talking about me behind my back. I felt like no one really understood my dream to reach women on so many levels while working to instill within them that you can work your business *and* have Jesus in your life. That Jesus and business can coexist.

So here are my nine tips that really helped me (and still do quite frankly) to keep moving forward, especially when I feel like I am not moving anywhere. Take five minutes, cry or punch it out and then take the "feel" out of your emotions, grab a Starbucks, throw on Beyonce and get back to work. I wrote this on January 14th, 2016, two days after I interviewed Domonique Price (whom you will read about shortly).

Thursday, January 14, 2016

We all get to this point one way or another in our journey as an entrepreneur. And if you haven't ever been there, then you haven't been hustling long enough. To be real, 100% transparent, I've had a week! Like an incredibly up and down, all over the place, crazy, ridiculous week. Some good stuff, some not so good stuff and some hard decisions to make. And since it has been "one of those weeks," I figured I know if I am feeling it, others are too. So why not write about it? I speak best when I write. It's like therapy.......

When looking at the bigger picture, I usually go back to why I started in the first place. Does that mean it fixes the situation right away? Nope. (In fact, I just bought a workout shirt three days ago that says that says NOPE. Clearly I was in a "NOPE" mood when I bought the shirt.) But when you can't see the bigger picture, when your vision is blurred because you've cried the mascara off your lashes and now it's in your eyes, take these nine things into consideration. These are the things I have to do when I have "one of those weeks."

Remember:

- *Everything in life is temporary, including the air you breathe. You'll will never have this day again, you may not have tomorrow and you can't change yesterday because it's gone. So why lose out on today? Live.*
- *Keep your emotions in check. I am not saying to ignore them, but don't let them over power you. That's the easiest way to convince yourself it's okay to give up. Tell yourself, it's NOT okay to give up.*
- *No one wants to come to your pity party. Every entrepreneur has "those days." Kind of like keeping your emotions in check, don't throw yourself a pity party. No one will show up.*
- *Positive propaganda is a must. I specifically don't have TV in my house. We have Apple TV to stream Netflix and Hulu, but zero cable TV. Watching the news is like dying a slow, painful death. And most of us keep coming back to that programming daily. Stop it! Read Forbes instead. Watch a podcast. Learn something on YouTube you've always wanted to try.*
- *Get yourself delivered from people. With 7.2 billion people on the plant, there's bound to be someone that rubs you the wrong way. Just deliver yourself from the situation. It's that simple.*
- *When you feel like giving up, your real supporters come out. There will be people lined up to see you fail. Pay no attention to them. Go to your "Fabulous Five" (as I call it.) You are the average of the five*

people you associate with most. Make sure those five are supporters and not haters (or even, worse silent haters = outwardly cheering you on but inside waiting for your pristine high heel to drop).

- *Failure is a stop on the way to success, it's not the destination. Only way you fail is if you give up.*
- *Success is a journey, not a destination. When I first started by launching my brand on Periscope, my first scope had one person. One. And one is all it took. I've built from there and I am not even the same person I was six months ago when #THEGIRLPRENEUR started.*
- *When you are feeling so low, when you are ready to call it and throw in the towel, when you can't make one more phone call, send one more email, can't hit "broadcast" on one more Periscope, ask yourself, "what's my alternative?" My alternative is scary enough to turn my frown upside down, put my heels back on and hustle like #thegirlpreneur I am.*

Fiercely You secret number six: Hell hath no fury like a woman in heels on a mission.

So a quick run-down on how I met Domonique is really nothing more than a God-divined appointment. Period. I have mentioned my life coach a couple of times in this book and during one of Cara's fabulous *Girl Code* workshops, I met Domonique. I was really so excited about getting to meet and know Domonique because not only was she in my workshop and I felt like we connected, she lived only thirty minutes away from me. Talk about divine appointments! During my entrepreneurial journey, I had lost a lot of friends, even in the church (and, yes, that does happen.) So when I found out she was a Jesus girl, an entrepreneur *and* she practically lived in my backyard, I had to meet up with her and connect. The more we talked and got to know each other, the more I truly valued her insight, her friendship and her journey as a Jesus girl in business. She is a 28-year-old fierce female entrepreneur who not only won Miss Oregon 2015 in the Miss USA pageant (while working as a full time lawyer), she was the youngest attorney ever to be on staff working for the Portland Trailblazers (professional NBA team.) Definitely get your power heels on because I know I needed them just to keep up on this interview.

A beauty queen in more ways than one

Domonique Price- Former Miss Oregon 2015, youngest attorney in Portland Trailblazer history to work for the team, lawyer and expert in trademark law, running her own business teaching entrepreneurs how to become Monguls.

Social Media
Instagram: @ domoniquep_esq
Periscope: @domoniquep_esq
Twitter: @domoniquep_esq
Facebook: Domonique Price
Website: www.domoniqueprice.com

So tell us about you, girl!
If Jesus and Erykah Badu had a baby it would be me. I am a self-proclaimed 28-year-old hippie, attorney helping entrepreneurs turn their business ideas into empires.

When did you realize you were an entrepreneur?
I have always been a lover of nice things. I started working when I was fifteen. My thought was, I always thought people should start off with a million dollars in life. You know, like that parable in the Bible where the three men are given "treasures" and two of the three "invest" them while the third goes and buries it. The first two multiplied their treasure and the third just had what he had because he buried it. I had the notion of creating a lot with the very little given; you can take what you have, God-given talents and all, invest it, you can build an empire.

So tell what it was like being Miss Oregon 2015. That has to be a ton of pressure! Beauty pageants and the beauty industry in general is a pretty tough judge. How did you do that for all those years and still keep your head on straight and your life pointed toward God?
Well, I did beauty pageants for five years. I have a ton of mixed emotions about it. My very first pageant, I worked my butt off. I was working out, I had a pageant coach, I was

eating pretty rigidly, etc. And I didn't win the title. I was devastated. I remember feeling like I let myself down. But then, after re-evaluation, something came over me. You can only compare you to yourself. It doesn't matter what others are doing. And whether I had the crown or not, I realized that I actually had exceeded my expectations.

How did pageants play a role in entrepreneurship for you?
Pageantry truly helped teach me the lessons of failing forward. Entrepreneurship is the exact same thing. More than likely, you won't get it right the first time. In fact, one of my favorite books by John Maxwell is called "Failing Forward." Sometimes to succeed, you have to fail forward. Even in failure, you have to assess those areas that need improvement. And it is a measure of you and only you, against yourself. No one else.

So when you are helping other entrepreneurs become "Monguls," how do you convey failing forward to them? What do you say to them?
I ask them what their alternative is. When you phrase it like that, it makes it real. Because what is your alternative? Only they know. Only I know what my alternative is if I don't continue to move forward with the plan and call that God has on my life. You have to take stock in what need to change and move forward.

So fast forward to present day. You win Miss Oregon 2015, you've failed forward after five years of pageant competition and you have the amazing opportunity to be in the Miss USA pageant. How did that feel?
After failing forward so many times, when I won, I was actually in disbelief. It's one thing in your mind and envisioning

it. It's a completely different thing to actually live it. It also resonated with me that I was not just representing myself, but I was representing all of those women that competed alongside me. It was truly a humbling experience.

How do you see yourself the way Jesus sees you?
I try to, every day, ask God to allow me to see myself the way He sees me. Think about this: there was this epic idea that God had: He created me to do what I am called to do, long before I was even called to do it. And this is the God and Creator of the universe, the God that created the universe in six days. You don't have time to *not* believe in yourself because He believes in you *that* much. I don't have time to be ordinary because I was created by an extraordinary God. That is mind blowing to me. I have only been on this earth for twenty-eight years but I have lived a very interesting life. This person with the crown, in a glamour gown, competing for Miss USA did not start off with type of focus and determination. I was born to a woman who didn't want to be a mom. I was born to a woman, that after having a child, decided I wasn't in her plans. After being passed around from family member to family member, I always felt abandoned. I felt like nobody wanted me. I felt like I had to make her love me. I tried to do well in school, etc. I always felt like I wasn't enough. With Jesus, *you are enough.*

Do you have a vision statement?
Helping people build generational wealth.

What keeps you inspired in your entrepreneurial journey?
Freedom. That is all. One word.

What fears have you dealt with over the course of your journey and how did you overcome them?
Dying full, and let me explain that. Martin Luther King, Jr had a speech that he had asked God to fill him up so that he could leave the world a better place. He was so afraid to be on his death-bed feeling like he still had more to do. I feel that there are certain things that God has placed me on this earth to accomplish. When I die, I want to enter into heaven and hear, "Well done, good and faithful servant."

I have overcome my fear through self talk. I talk to myself a lot! You might be driving next to me but don't be alarmed- I am just in full blown conversation with myself.

What advice do you have for other female entrepreneurs out there?
Picture yourself as if you were you're daughter. What would you say to her? That's how I push myself.

What have you learned as a Jesus girl and a business woman?
That I am still navigating. It wasn't up until this past year that I learned that God and business don't have to be exclusive separately. They are one in the same. You need to have them exclusively together.

What do you do every single day?
I would really like that answer to be "pray." But it's not. I drink water every single day because I don't believe in ever being thirsty. I am working on my need for daily prayer to be just as essential as my routine with water. That is the honest truth.

What has helped keep you disciplined in your business?
My desire to be a multi-millionaire. It helps me on the days that I have a difficult client. It helps me when I think about staying out of the 9-5. It keeps me on track when I don't want to work. It then shifts my mindset to focusing on the freedom, the ability to travel and financial security. Then I get up and go.

So whether you *feel* like it or not, you have to show up to go up. You may not feel like wearing the crown and strutting around in your heels. But as Joyce Meyer always says, "You have to do what you know is right and eventually your feelings will catch up." Just slip the heels on, throw that crown up there and walk proudly.......even if you don't *feel* like it.

Coffee Thoughts:

1. What is one thing you are going to commit to showing up to this week in your business?

____
____
____
____
____

2. What is one thing that you are going to do to pick yourself back up when you don't feel like putting the crown and heels back on?

____
____
____
____
____

3. What is one area of your business where you are going to persevere?

____
____
____
____
____

CHAPTER 7

WHEN YOU CAN AFFORD IT, YOU HIRE YOUR WEAKNESSES. DON'T BE YOUR WEAKNESS.

"As soon as you are able, hire your weaknesses."

–Sara Blakely, Founder of Spanx

So I would say that out of all the quotes I have put down in this book, this is probably one of my favorites. Why? Because when we all start out as entrepreneurs, we are the "one-woman show." We end up having to do it all to get things off the ground. But what I love about this quote is that it really embodies the message that we do not have to be perfect. Sure, in the beginning it is hard. There are tons of things that have happened in my business, in the businesses of the other women that you have read and are reading about and, more than likely, there are things in your business that are just not your forte. And you know what? That is 100% okay. So stop worrying about having to have it all figured out.

I am a total type A personality and so naturally I want to have my hands into everything, my brain wrapped around it all and have it all figured out before I even get to the destination. The reality is, I don't have it all figured out and neither will you. So get used to it and get comfortable with it. Now, that doesn't mean you get to stop learning. In fact, pick up all that you can along the way, but don't beat yourself up for not being able to know it all. To be perfectly honest, although networking via social media is probably one of my strongest traits (I absolutely love it and have met some of the most incredible people via social media), I would say I am terrible at the technical media side of things, as in the inner workings of it. My website? I didn't build it. Truth be told, I don't even post my own blog posts. I have someone else do that for me because it would take me twice as long to figure it all out. My book launch, the cover, the design, etc. all done outside of my scope. I hired someone to do that too. But here is where I will get brutally honest.

Hiring outside help is no excuse to stop learning. Hiring someone out of laziness is an excuse that you cannot use. Let's get clear about that. What do I mean? I mean that just because you may not be good at something doesn't mean that you shouldn't necessarily know how things work. There are many ways that you can learn something quickly.

YouTube, HELLO! "Google University." It's called the Internet.

Does that mean you need to be an expert? No, not at all. I am simply saying don't use the excuse of not knowing how to do something as a reason to not learn it. The worst thing you can do to yourself is to discontinue being a student. I will use myself as an example.

By the time this book is released I will be finished (or close to finishing) the Millennial Rich Girl program with Alex Wolf, Creator of #Bossbabe. It is a program that works with female entrepreneurs on building online systems that help streamline cash flow. It is the inner workings of building sites, technology at your fingertips and how to maximize those avenues so that you can maximize your time. I needed to learn how to do that stuff and I had been following Alex since the beginning of the #Bossbabe movement, so naturally that is why I chose to work with her. Plus, she is just a cool chick that I developed a relationship with via social media over time. But, the point is, I knew I needed to be up to date. And sometimes, you will need to take a deep dive into things so that you can eventually free up your time and space. Time is the one thing that once it's gone, it's gone. You can't get it back. The best investment you can make is in yourself. So never use hiring help as an excuse to minimize your learning and expansion of knowledge. I want to make sure I am clear on that.

The thief of defeat

Let's talk about this for a minute. If we know that in John 10:10 that the "thief comes only to steal and kill and destroy" we know we need to be on guard. The enemy will use whatever means necessary, whether that be the feelings of imperfection, guilt, condemnation, lack of knowledge, lack of skill, lack of support, etc. to make us feel as though the call on our life is not worth pursuing. You have to understand that the furthering of His kingdom in any way, shape or form is going to be met with opposition. We are going to feel the weight of that pressure of having to have it all done, figured out or completed of our own accord. In what may feel like the utmost chaotic point in your business, ask yourself: what do I need to do differently in order to not lose the vision, not lose the mission and crumble under the pressure? What can I outsource? What can I finish myself? If you feel yourself at that breaking point within your business, the best thing to do is stop what you are doing and reassess. When we don't stop and reassess what we are doing, we are doing nothing other than allowing the thief of defeat into our mind and our business. And worse, we end up running in circles. You have to be on your highest guard and recognize the enemy before he has a chance to settle in and get you running in circles you don't need to be running.

Not to be a "Debbie downer" but statistically, according to Forbes, eight of ten business or entrepreneurs fail within the first eighteen months of starting up or launching. Now although I agree with Forbes in that a huge piece of that is often times business owners and entrepreneurs lose touch with the voice of the customer, I would also argue and say it is really because we lose touch with ourselves. We lose sight of the *why*. We forget why we started. We allowed the fear, the anxiety, the hiccups, the setbacks, or the bumpy road to derail us. And when we are derailed, our customers and clients become derailed as well. Customers and clients can feel that without words even really needing to be spoken. Thus, it could lead to the business collapsing (if we let it.) There is a quote that I absolutely love by Jim Rohn that depicts so pointedly the difference between having vigilance in our business to avoid defeat versus being vigilant so we aren't defeating ourselves. He says, "Beware of the thief on the street that is after your purse, but also beware of the thief that is in your mind that's after your promise." When you feel yourself get to that point, assess. Do I need to hire help? What can I delegate? What do I need to change? The worst thing you can do it give up on what you've already started.

Embrace that you are perfect in your imperfection

Before I get to my next interview, which is someone that I have known for over a decade and I am super excited to share her journey with you, I want to talk about the perfectness of imperfection. First and foremost, as a Jesus girl, it took me a long time to understand that I am perfect in my imperfection. I am covered by grace and loved by the King of Kings. I am a princess in His eyes. After a ten year battle with depression and anxiety, my overall mission is to help other women through their journeys as entrepreneurs because during my journey in becoming an entrepreneur, I spent years suppressing my God given entrepreneurial spirit. I never embraced my imperfections until I realized I knew I was right in Jesus and that I had God given talents that needed to be used to further His kingdom. Before I arrived at that point though, I let other people around me make me feel like my dreams weren't worth pursuing. I worked for a company that had actually told me (verbatim), "this is not a place in which you are free to exercise your entrepreneurial spirit." I used to think that Jesus and my business couldn't be one in the same. I felt awkward that my husband was a worship Pastor that everyone knew, while I sat in the shadows of the congregation. I always felt judged, which was just the enemy planting seeds and lies into my mind that I was worth less than I really was.

Fiercely You secret number seven: Transformation takes dedication.

This next interview is with one of my dearest friends and someone who has supported me throughout my corporate career, my journey as a mom, an entrepreneur and has helped bring my health back to life after I spent three years in and out of hospitals and surgeries. We met in church over a decade ago. She is a corporate queen managing multi-million dollar assets, is an entrepreneur herself running two businesses on the side and a Tough Mudder chick. This woman does not mess around and I love her for it. I think the biggest reason I just clicked with her is she was not afraid to speak her mind, even as a Jesus girl. Sometimes I think there is a misconception that just because Jesus is involved in our businesses, we can't be who we really are. Couldn't be further from the truth. Be who you are because that is exactly how God created you to be. So hang on tight for this fierce female and her journey in entrepreneurship and fitness. It's a good one.

Social Media
Twitter: @fitafter40chick
Instagram: @fitafter40chick
SnapChat: @kimberlyboard
Facebook: fitafter40chick
Periscope: @kimberlyboard

So tell us about yourself!
Well, I am a 47-year-old, corporate executive with an entrepreneur heart, who is very passionate about health and fitness. So much so, that I started my own business and brand to be able to help other people take control of their own health and fitness.

When did you realize you were an entrepreneur?
I realized I was an entrepreneur when I fell in love with my network marketing business. I realized it was my future and I was ready to make it work.

As a mom, a wife, a corporate executive, etc.—how has that played a role in your business?
Oh, that plays a huge role in my business. When I am working on my business, which is 24/7, I always have them at the forefront. They are my WHY. And although I only have sons, I don't have daughters, I want them to understand that they do not have to rely on someone else in order to make their life great. They are my reason for doing what I do.

How do you see yourself as Jesus would see you?
That's funny that you ask me that. I have been thinking about that a lot lately. I think He wants me to please Him, but as woman who has had to overcome a lot and really put a lot of faith into knowing that He has guided me through the process. The process of my brand has been a long process. It started about ten years ago, it came to fruition just last year in 2015. When I realized I wanted to help other people and it was also just as long a process of digging deep within myself and learning to be unapologetically me.

So ten years, to create fitafter40chick?
Yes. So ten years ago, my husband decided to change his life and I watched him and helped him through that. He decided to take a fitness path and he had always been athletic. I never was. I was always the heaviest girl in class....I couldn't even run once around the track in gym class. I was that girl who hated going to gym class because it was always brutally embarrassing. So when I started the brand, immediately I was like, "umm, I am not this person." But, we started to do events, I started to follow along and ride my bike. It took me a long time to be able to keep up with the group.

Then, I found I had this really extremely high blood pressure. I could feel the pressure in my chest, to the point of not being able to breathe. I went to the doctor and he was like "oh, yeah you need to take medication for this." I decided right then and there that I was going to fix this with exercise. I then went to becoming "pescitorian" which means we don't eat meat but we eat fish or seafood and only if we catch it. That way we know exactly what we are eating and ingesting. No chemicals.

Through trial and error and cardio and weights, I was finally able to get my blood pressure down to a very normal level. It has remained there at a normal level for the last four years. I realized through the process that being athletic doesn't mean you are a certain size or a certain type of person. Being athletic is just being able to do it. Walk around the block! My mantra is athletes come in all shapes and sizes. I don't ever want anyone to think that just because they weren't born athletic doesn't mean they can't become that. Where they are and where they can be doesn't matter—- their past doesn't matter, what they had for dinner last night doesn't matter, it just matters that they can start from where ever they are at.

Do you have a mission statement or vision statement? How did you come up with?

I aspire to help others learn to enjoy health and fitness at any age and learn that you do not have to "break the tape" to win. I came up with it because that was something that I struggled with, not only mentally for a long time, but physically as well on my fitness journey. I had to learn that I am only in competition with myself.

What inspires you the most in your entrepreneurial journey?

There are so many things that inspire me. And since I am still sometimes figuring things out, other people's successes inspire me. Other entrepreneurial journeys and successes inspire me. The little things that happen every day are a big deal to me. Something that someone else might walk by and miss, to me, are so important. Those are a big deal.

What fears do you have and how did you (or how do you) overcome them?

My biggest fear with fitafer40chick is that somebody will try to knock me down and I just have to know that those people are going to be around. Those people are always going to be there. I am always learning how to handle those people and situations. I use it to propel and fuel me rather than paralyze me with fear. "Haters gonna hate" and I just have to learn that I don't drink "haterade." I think another fear I have is that the people I work with and help, that are looking to me and trusting me on their journey, I don't want to let them down.

What is the number one thing that you have learned in your in your journey as Jesus girl in business?

To probably just patient with the process and trust that the Lord has His hand both IN and ON the process. I have to realize that it is not going to happen over night. Building a brand and international networking marketing business from home is not an overnight thing. He will put the right people in my path. And, if He closes a door, I can't just go back and try to bust it open. I have to be patient for what is coming in my business. It took me ten years just to get to "fitafter40chick." The process is worth it though.

What is one thing you do every single day?

I do a lot of things every single day. The most important of those is pray. I pray every day because it keeps me grounded. It keeps me on the right path. When I pray I don't want it to be about me. I want people to know that it, the whole process and journey, is bigger than just "fitafter40chick."

How do you stay disciplined in your business?
Ahhh, that is a hard question! You are always getting pulled in different directions. You have to designate time to certain things, and I have a certain time of day that I designate to my business....nothing else. I have certain times, every single day, seven days a week that are strictly dedicated to my business. It is the same thing with my workouts. It's a 4am *non- negotiable.* After the gym, it is time spent with God and then on my business. Each afternoon, I have an hour that I spend on my business. When I get home from the office, the evening time is business hours for my brand and I. I actually dream about my business, even when I sleep....it drives me in all areas in my life. I constantly ask myself, "is this going to benefit me and/or business?" And if the answer is "no" then I simply don't do it. I am saying "NO" now so I can say "YES" later.

Okay, ladies, so I have a little homework for you on this one. What I really want you to think about today and the rest of the week is one thing that you are going to do to get clarity on what you need to do in order to get to where you want to go. Like Kimberly said above, it is easy to get pulled into a million different directions. So I want you to take the next few pages and really write out what you are going to do to narrow some things down and get specific. Don't allow the enemy to have a foothold in your mind and allow it to get clouded with a bunch of noise. Let's get clear with some things. And if you can afford it, hire those weaknesses.

Coffee Thoughts:

1. What is one thing in my business I can either hire or barter with someone else to do for me, so I can focus on my business the best way I can?

____
____
____
____
____

2. What is one ***new*** thing I am going to learn how to do this week in my business? (Whether that be a 'How To' Podcast, learn Periscope, learn how to upload videos to my YouTube Channel or blog, etc). Pick one thing and stick to it. Put a date of completion on it.

____
____
____
____
____

3. What is one negative thought I am going to let go of, whether it be about myself or my business, and turn that into a positive thought?

____
____

4. How do I think Jesus sees me versus how I see myself?

5. What is one "imperfection" I am going to let go of and give over to God?

CHAPTER 8

THE MODERN DAY PROVERBS 31 GIRL.

"For she is clothed in strength and dignity and she laughs without fear of the future."

Proverbs 31:25 (NIV).

I have been dying to break this down in the modern day woman world.....you have no idea. First of all, why in the world it took me over a decade to get this verse engrained in my head and my heart is beyond me. If there is one thing that you take away from this chapter, I want it to be this verse. Seriously. Don't wait over a decade like I did to realize that God's best is waiting for you.

Description of a "Worthy" Woman

Funny story about Proverbs chapter 31. And this is just me being real. When my husband and I were not as financially sound as we are now, I would literally take Proverbs 31:17,

"She equips herself with strength [spiritual, mental, and physical fitness for her God given task]..." (AMP) and use that to justify why I needed to *at least* be able to get my hair done. See I am not a natural blonde. I absolutely love being a blonde, but we as fierce females all know, being a blonde immediately means upkeep. It's not the cheapest thing in the world to do (but getting your hair done sure feels awesome.) I'd say something like, "Well, babe, if I am going to be in front of people, working in business, which is my God-given talent, I need to make sure my hair is on point." Talk about taking scripture and twisting it (although it worked.) Now we just budget for that a month or so in advance, but yes, I was that girl trying to justify getting my hair done with the Word of God.

Unpacking the woman

But here is where I want to unpack this. And I thought about not including a chapter specifically referencing this portion of the Bible but as a fierce female myself, and for all the fierce females out there reading this, I felt like I needed to. I am going to be 100% honest and say when I read Proverbs 31 verbatim, I had a hard time digesting it all. Especially when I became a mother. I felt like this chapter was a chapter depicting the "mom, wife, servant, etc. that must stay home to cook, clean and raise children." I felt incredibly guilty because at the time I had had my first child, Isaac, and I was most definitely not ready to be a mom. My husband and I had only been married two months, we had just closed escrow on our condominium and two days after getting the keys, we found out we were going to have a baby. I would be further lying if I said I wasn't ticked off. Yes, I was that wife giving my husband the glare of "you……you did this to me….." Now, over time, obviously that feeling has subsided and I've adjusted to motherhood, but I held on to the guilt of not wanting to be a stay at home mom for years. It tormented me actually. I remember thinking, "Lord what the heck is wrong with me for not wanting to be with my children? Did I miss that gene somewhere in the creation of my life?"

From the time I was a young teenager, I knew I wanted to be in business. I knew I wanted to be the CEO of ME. So naturally when I found out I was pregnant, I had the attitude of "well, this is not in my plans." It really wasn't, at least not *that* early into our marriage. Now everything being hindsight, you know the 20/20 vision you get after a life storm, I see why everything happened the way it did. Shortly after having my second son, I was plagued with a litany of health issues with my reproductive system. After three years of intense pain, four laparoscopic surgeries, a mountain of medical bills and recovery time, I finally had to have a full hysterectomy at the age of thirty-one due to massive fibroids, endometriosis, ovarian cysts and scarred tissue. Needless to say, it is a miracle my children were not only born healthy, but that God decided to bless me with them when He did.

But it still didn't take away the feelings that I had (and sometimes still wrestle with) in terms of being a "Proverbs 31" mom and wife. I was wrestling with the infamous "Proverbs 31" woman that I felt was always stifling who I really was. And the more I felt ridden with guilt, the more depressed I became. I became depressed about wanting to be a Jesus girl in business, I felt guilty about not wanting to stay home with my children and rising "also while it is still night and give food to her household and assign takes to her maids" (AMP). I wanted to be a power house in business; not cook and clean. (And I'll be brutally honest, I still hate cooking....don't mind the cleaning part though.) I just couldn't get my brain wrapped around why I couldn't be "this woman."

So of course, I started to do some research and came across this article in *LifeWay* that was written by a woman named Vicki Courtney. Now before I give account of it, which I think is very applicable to the modern day woman, I want to be clear that the book of Proverbs was actually written by King Solomon. And Solomon, as we know, had like a billion wives. Some believe that the Proverbs 31 woman is a composite of all the women Solomon had as wives. Some literally take the Proverbs 31 woman to heart and do their best to follow it to the letter of law (yes, there are those that do and there is no shame in that either.) Some believe the whole chapter is a metaphor, while some take the chapter in bits and pieces. Really the chapter is a depiction of King Solomon's mom; which let's face it, none of us are like that today. So can we agree to kind of just throw this "perfect Proverbs 31 woman" out the window for a minute? Good.

So let's get to this blog post that I thought was just phenomenal from *LifeWay*. She breaks down the whole "Proverbs 31" woman in a way that made so much sense to me. She states and gives recognition that in the Bible the Proverbs 31 woman is real, she breaks down how we apply that woman to ourselves today. And of course, the moment

I read it in that light, I fell in love with the concept and realness it portrayed. She breaks down that the very core of a virtuous woman is her devotion to the Lord. It's the number one quality in a woman that trumps all the others. Proverbs 31:30 says (AMP), "Charm and grace are deceptive, and [superficial] beauty is vain. But a woman who fears the Lord [reverently worshipping, obeying, serving, and trusting Him with awe-filled respect] she shall be praised." I want you to really let that sink in. Let that seep into the depths of your soul.

A woman that has reverential fear of the Lord? That is a women who is no door mat. That is a woman who has no weak will, is strong in her God-given strengths and doesn't ignore and suppress them. That woman may look like a divorced mom of four with two jobs or a young twenty-year-old woman with tattoos and piercings working at a restaurant with a smile on her face. It may be a mom going back to school to finish her degree in cosmetology or a woman homeschooling her children. Or it may be a woman who once was a girl with the dreams of being her own boss, running an international business and writing a book at the same time. My point? You can't stereotype the plan in place that God has already set in motion over your life. You are who you are in Him. Anything less than living out the call He has placed on your life is just noise.

It took me forever to arrive at that realization. I ignored the call on my life to be a Jesus girl who reaches women in the business realm as an author, speaker and teacher in business. I believed that there was no way that Jesus and business could function together. As in the two couldn't work together or be intertwined. Really that was just the enemy, once again, seeping into the deepest crevices of my mind and heart, making me feel and believe that I wasn't good enough to do either of those things. I allowed myself to be chained to a desk for twelve years in the corporate world because I thought, well, if I can't do both, then I'll at least live out my dream of working business and having that big corner office. It was one of the biggest mistakes of my life. But I have been redeemed. I am walking, living, breathing proof that when He instills the dreams and desires within your heart that they can and will come to fruition. It's like Jessika mentioned in her interview in the few chapters previous, "do not be afraid to bring anything to Him first." I really want you to get that. Bring it to Him first. Whatever it is you are going for, whatever you know God has called you to do, don't wait to bring it to Him. Don't make it the last thing you bring to Him. Don't do it somewhere in the middle. If you want it, bring it to Him first. He'll figure out the rest. That I know for sure to be true in my own life.

Fiercely You secret number eight: The Proverbs 31 woman does exist. She is YOU. Own you because you are perfect in Him.

This next interview is just a flat out phenomenal one. Her name is Tiphani Montgomery. And the story in how I met her is quite interesting. And the story of how she ended up in my book is even better (and nothing short of God doing His thing.)

I met Tiphani via Periscope somewhere around August of 2015. That was about the time I started to jump on the Periscope train and became obsessed with reaching as many women as possible with my message. Tiphani's charisma was magnetic. She was so confident and sure of not only herself as a business woman, but she was a totally 100% sold out for Jesus. I would listen to her prayer scopes (which are phenomenal by the way), listen to her breakdown scripture and just knock a message out of the park. In fact, she was one of the people that really got me thinking about writing a book. She also was the first one that encouraged me to start Periscoping and "jump in and just do it." Over time, I just kept listening and sharing her content because it was so profound and so well communicated. So naturally, when I started to work on the book, I thought, I have to have Tiphani as one of my interviewees. I reached out to Tiphani via email the week between Christmas and New Year's in hopes to snag some time to chat with her and get the interview done. About three weeks went by and I hadn't heard anything. I was a little bummed but knowing that God's plan is the master plan, I let it go gracefully (plus, I knew she was a *very* busy woman.) So remember my friend Domonique? You are going to love this. This is where God's plan is perfect in every way.

When Domonique and I had scheduled our time to meet up and have dinner and do the interview, it was a Wednesday night. We had to do it on Wednesday because she was leaving for a conference in Chicago early that next day. I said, "Done. Let's meet at Joey's in Southcenter before you have to leave then."

So the two of us met up for dinner, had a fantastic interview and a phenomenal dinner. We needed to wrap up so Domonique could pick up her phone at the Apple store and as we were paying our bill to leave, I popped on my phone real quick to check Facebook and saw a quote Tiphani had posted. I said, somewhat quietly, "Oh Tiphani is dropping gems again." Domonique looked at me and said, "Tiphani? Tiphani Montgomery?" I said, "Yes." Domonique just looked at me and said, "That's who I am meeting in Chicago tomorrow for the conference." *Mic drop.*

Like are you kidding me? So, here I was sitting thinking, "Oh well, it would have been awesome to feature Tiphani, but I get it, she is busy, she has a million things going on. Out of the 7.2 billion people on the planet, what are the odds that I was sitting having dinner with Tiphani's friend (and attorney) the day before she was going to leave where the two of them were going to meet up for a conference? You can't tell me that is not a God thing. Period.

So, curl up and get comfortable for this dynamic interview I had with Tiphani Montgomery, bestselling author, founder and executive director of the non-profit organization called "Knocked Up, Now What," entrepreneur, mom and child of God.

Social Media
Periscope: @tiphanimontgomery
Twitter: @Tiphani_M
Instagram: @tiphanimontgomery
Facebook (Fan Page): Tiphani Montgomery
Website: www.tiphanimontgomery.com

So tell us about you!
When I was twelve, they told me I was stupid and prescribed 'smart pills' (aka Ritalin) to wrestle my brain into a state of submission. I fed them to my dog, Zeus. They worked liked a charm. When I was twenty-one, they told me I'd never amount to anything, so I took my daughter, moved to a new state and self-published a book of poetry....which I sold from the behind the bar where I mixed drinks and hustled tips. When I was twenty-five, my college GPA was an abysmal 0.0, so I dropped out. Wrote my first (of four novels) in two and a half months and from there, landed on the Essence Magazine best seller list seven separate times-including the #1 spot. Today, nobody calls me stupid and I live to tell the tale.

Your story is incredible. Probably one of the biggest reasons I started following your journey and became hooked on your Periscopes. God has shaped you through that..... talk about that a little bit.
When people start serving God, they stop at the "I love God" part. I think that is what really changed my perspective and moved me to a different position. I get up every day to serve God. The cells in my body carry duties of power. Success was not an option for me either. I started to embody that

is was NOT an option. That if I got a "no" somewhere, I needed to get a "yes" somewhere else.

As a mom at a young age, writing your first of four novels in a two-month span, how did you balance all of that?
I think it's important to schedule everything and all your time out. Your gym is scheduled, your push-ups are scheduled, your prayer time is scheduled. Everything has a time and place. As an entrepreneur, you are not in college, you cannot freestyle that stuff. You have to implement that stuff. That's like the only thing I learned in school. I schedule out my time to pray, studying my bible, my marketing, schedule time with your children. Keep your focus on what is *scheduled.* So when my daughter was sleeping (when she was younger) I would write when she was finally asleep for the night. 10pm-2am was my schedule for writing and that was a hard line.

How do you see yourself as Jesus sees you?
Ummm, I think I see love. He overwhelmingly loves me. It's not a surface-y love. That is really it. That is all I need to keep pushing forward.

Do you have a mission/vision statement? If so, what is it?
I don't. I don't know if it's right or wrong to have a mission statement. I know that I am so weird and creative, and peculiar. I always feel like God has me on a mission. I do know at the core, I am here to heal the sick, cast out demons and raise the dead. My mission changes from year to year, but I go where God tells me to go.

What inspires you the most in your entrepreneurial journey?
Not having a 9-5, I don't have an option to *not* make this work. I am a servant by nature. Anything I've ever done in life, I am going to help someone. If someone needs help writing a book, I am going to help them. What inspires me is that this *has* to work. I am not going to marry a rich man. I learned early in life. I have two children and I don't want to rely on a man and a 9-5.

What fears do you have and how do you (or have you) overcome them?
I am sure I have fears every single day. Overall, it is so easy for me to put things into perspective. While I may have fears, I don't really know what they are specifically. I follow up with the fear immediately and that translates into overcoming it, quickly.

What advice do you have for woman who may struggle with holding on to their unshakable WHY?
First of all, I don't think everyone should be an entrepreneur. If you have been wavering for five to ten years, then it may not be for you. That's okay. If you have been a "waiter,"

waiting for the right time, the right place, then being an entrepreneur may not be the path for you. However, as an entrepreneur, surround yourself with other entrepreneurs that are successful. For example, when I surrounded myself around successful people and heard how easy it was to get out....out of my situation...my mind shifted. The Bible says that we are the covered by the blood of the Lamb.

What is the number one thing you have learned in your journey as a Jesus girl and a woman in business?
That number one thing is power. I did not understand how powerful I was as a believer in Jesus Christ. The Kingdom of God is not just in words, but in demonstration. Operating in the gift of (fill in the blank of what your gift is) words, business, works, etc. Prophetic words. I am operating in the market place in the work I am passionate about. I am in the market place not just in words but in my demonstration of Jesus Christ.

What is one thing you do every single day?
I pray every day. And not just a "good morning" prayer but a one to two hours a day. I check my email every day. Sometimes I think I am a part time "email answerer." I have not delegated that out yet.

How do you stay disciplined in your business?
Again, I go back to there is no other option for me. I cannot have a 9-5, so I have to stay disciplined. It's like anyone else with a 9-5 or a career of some sort right? Nobody thinks twice about going to work. They set their alarm clock. They are there at their place of work and arrive to their jobs on time. I am the same way. I do not have a plan B.

Phew! Did ya'll get all of that?! Tiphani is right on the money though. As hard of a realization as that may be for some to process, she's right. We have to operate in more than just words, but demonstration. We have to accept that failure is not an option, especially as we are daughters of Jesus. There is power in your purpose. There is an array of gifts you have as a woman and in who God created you to be. Don't ignore that. We cannot look at our future(s) and curl up in fear. We have to look at it, face it straight on and laugh in the face of fear knowing we have a God that is so much bigger than any problem or hang up we'll ever face in our businesses. You are made to be who you are, so don't let the illusion of who you should be derail you from who you are and where you are meant to go.

Coffee Thoughts:

1. What is my number one fear that I am going to hand over to God this week?

____

____

____

____

____

2. What is the biggest lie the enemy has been holding over me that I am letting go of this week?

____

____

____

____

____

3. I have power in my purpose. What is one way I am going to demonstrate that power this week?

____

____

____

____

____

CHAPTER 9

BEING A MODERN DAY RUTH

"Life isn't about finding yourself. Life is about creating yourself."

–George Bernard Shaw

So, I know we just visited the whole Proverbs 31 woman thing and broke that down. In speaking with all of the women and female entrepreneurs I talk with on a daily basis, there always seems to be one common denominator. There is this overwhelming, heavy feeling of "having to do it all" and be superwoman, all while running a business.

There is an increasingly heavier weighted pressure when we become moms because we have that much more to do in terms of responsibility and less time in which to do it.....a lot less time. There is this false sense that being a Proverbs 31 woman is what we *have* to become, which again let's remind ourselves, ladies, it's not all about doing your husband's laundry, cooking, cleaning, taking care of the children solely, etc. All of those things are good but, it doesn't make you a horrible mom, parent or woman if your desires lie elsewhere outside the home either.

I know I wrestled with that for years. At first, I didn't even want to be home. I hated the idea of being a stay-at-home parent honestly. But as God softened my heart, opened my ears, cleared my mind and started to really work on me, I realized that the whole Proverbs 31 wife thing was not about being the "submissive" wife (for lack of a better term). It was simply about having that reverential fear of the Lord and keeping that as my number one character trait.

Needless to say, I failed at that miserably in the past, but have come to grips with it now and understand what God is asking of me and how He is asking me to do it. You can be a mom and a business woman. You can be a student and a business woman. You can be a wife that likes to cook and run an international business from your home. You can go back to school and get your degree and do laundry. You can, and are *allowed* and CALLED to be you. I can be a Pastor's wife, running an international network marketing business, while writing books, helping other women to do the same, all from my home. I could do that all from an office if I chose to as well. And some women do. And guess what?! That is just fine too! No one should create the space in which you operate and work except you and Jesus. It's up to you two to figure that out.

What would Ruth say?

I love the idea of being a "Modern Day Ruth." I say that not because we should all go off and marry someone we've never met. Honestly, I say to my husband (more often times than not), I am not sure I would have survived those times. Yikes. But there is something about Ruth that I just love. I love that Ruth, throughout her whole journey and throughout her life in the Bible, had an open mind and a teachable spirit. It was like she had this unbelievable, unwavering faithfulness in times throughout her life where she couldn't see or know the outcome. I mean, I freak out if I can't see how the barista is writing out my drink on the cup at Starbucks. I would be passed out in shock if God had me marry some man I had never met! Sometimes, I think the women in the Bible would just laugh at what we Jesus girls freak out over these days.

Ruth is one of those women in the Bible that you just look at and see God taking her whole life in the direction He had foreordained. He works out His perfect plan on her life. Why? Because she had an open mind and teachable spirit. She is a true example of what it looks like when we just trust the will God has for our lives. I picture a modern day Ruth, standing up at a podium looking all chic and savvy, killing it in some Louboutins saying, "Ladies, get it together! If I can do this, so can you. Just move aside and let God do His thing." And she'd have the whole conference room at a standing ovation cheering her on because of her boldness. She'd probably run the business world, just sayin'. Why? Because she is fearless. She knows she has a God bigger than any problem, situation or fear that could ever come her way. And then I sit back and say to myself, "Dang, I can't even trust a barista to make my coffee?"

We have to get better about being a modern day Ruth in our businesses. At the end of the day, we aren't in control. God is. Think about how much easier it would be to get to that end goal, that next step in your business, that next promotion or that next level if we just had an open mind and teachable spirit like Ruth? It sounds so easy to do, but why is it so hard? I struggle with it *still* sometimes. Sometimes I will be on my way to pick up my boys from school and just start talking out loud to God saying stuff like, "God why can I not hand this over? You've done it before, so why am I not moving aside and letting you do it again?" We get so consumed with being in the driver's seat, having to do it all, be everything to everyone that all we end up really doing is hurting ourselves (and sometimes the loved ones around us.) Believe me, been there, done that and the husband wasn't thrilled about getting the T-shirt on that one either. If a woman like Ruth can entrust God with her *entire* life (which we should be doing anyway), don't you think we at least owe it to ourselves to trust God with our businesses? I mean after all, He is the one who gave us the desires, the dreams, the ambitions and the hopes, right? Don't you think it's time you be that modern day Ruth and hand your business over to God? Like for real this time?

Fiercely You secret number nine: It was never yours to begin with.

This was, and still is sometimes, the hardest thing I have to come to grips with as a fierce female and Jesus girl in business. The business is never really mine. God is using me to fulfill His ultimate plan. I am a vessel for Him. All the money, the "stuff," the recognition is never ours to begin with. So often we seek approval from our peers and colleagues, our business partners and sometimes even our spouses, but the only recognition that matters at the end of the day is the recognition He gives us. Don't get me wrong. Everyone needs and deserves recognition. In fact, statics show that those who receive praise and positive words of encouragement are 47% more likely to produce and have a more enjoyable work environment and less likely to leave companies simply because they feel valued and appreciated. There is a very important element to that in your business.

What I am talking about though is, when the fame hits, when the money starts really flowing in, when things are "firing on all cylinders," it is He who made it happen. It is not us. And yet, we often forget that. And what is so interesting as well, is when things aren't going well in our businesses, we *still* seek approval, affirmation and recognition from all the wrong channels. We go to Facebook to see how many people have commented or "liked" our posts, we turn to "how many new followers do I have today" or to others within our business to fill that hole, that empty space. Now, let me clarify. I am not talking about supporting each other in the business arena. You need that. You most certainly need that community. But what I am referring to is when things get really tough, when you can't make one more phone call, when you can't stand to send out one more email or take one more conference call, turn to Him instead for the validation and direction; not to Facebook or someone else. There is no other verse in the Bible that says it better than Philippians 4:6 (AMP), "Do not be anxious *or* worried about anything, but in everything [every circumstance and situation] by prayer and petition with thanksgiving continue to make your [specific] requests known to God."

Do you get how powerful that really is? I mean really? Do you understand that this is the easiest thing to do, yet the hardest one to actually see through? I know because I have been there. Nothing in this whole book, no situation, no roadblock, no fear that has been described are things or situations I haven't been through myself. And I go back to this. I simply didn't make my requests, my specific requests, known to God *first.* Don't make the requests known part way through or toward the end, make your requests the very first thing you do and bring it to God. Tell Him exactly what you are looking for, tell Him exactly where you want to go, and tell Him what you need. Let me give you an example. Every single woman that I have interviewed in this book are people that I prayed for specifically to feature. I actually prayed specifically for Kim Garst to be one of the people featured in this book. I had no clue what her life looked like outside of Periscope, I had no idea if she'd even respond to my request. But on the day that I was getting ready to send her the request to ask for an interview, I prayed over my message before I even wrote it out. And now thinking back to it, the message was so simple, so short, but it was specific. But I prayed over it *first.* Tiphani was another one I prayed for specifically. I prayed very specifically to feature her because I know her heart for Jesus. I knew it needed to be shared. So when the interview happened the way that it did, I knew it was nothing short of that being a God thing. That was totally Him. That was *nothing* of me. Get fierce with those wants and desires in your business. You will be absolutely blown away at what God can do.

The Shark Tank

Okay, so this next fierce female I am jumping out of my Louboutins to bring to you. Honestly, this whole story of how we met and became connected is, yet again, nothing short of a God thing. So I will rewind about a year and a half ago when I was at a networking event at the Tacoma Convention and Trade Center. I was working in a booth promoting my business and doing a meet and greet with potential customers and brand partners. About three hundred yards away, I saw this cute little green apron with white polka dots on it and I saw there were pickles being sampled out. Anyone who knows me well, knows I absolutely *love* pickles. Like love them! So in between meet and greets, I told my other business partners I was going to take a stroll down to the pickle booth and grab a sample. I mean come on, who doesn't like free, right? As I approached the booth, I saw the sign that said, "As seen on *Shark Tank*." So of course, immediately I am drawn in because Shark Tank and Undercover Boss are my two absolute favorite shows. I walked up, grabbed a few of the different flavors of pickles and my mouth just froze. I couldn't even muster up the courage to ask this complete stranger about her experience on *Shark Tank*. Like, what the heck had just come over me? This wasn't my first rodeo. I am a business woman. I can talk to anyone. But I couldn't bring myself to ask the question, "OMG, what was it like being on *Shark Tank*?" I still don't know why to this day I couldn't ask the question, but I went home that night and immediately watched the YouTube episode she was featured on. Season five, episode one. The season premiere of *Shark Tank* had Mrs. Aly Cullinane and her business partner (at the time) Lynne presenting "Lynne's Pickles" to the sharks themselves. The episode was a phenomenal episode and very well done, if I do to say so myself. I mean, we all know how the sharks can be right? It was kind of cool to be able to tell my husband, she was there at the networking event. I worked with a celebrity that day.

Fast forward seventeen months later, my husband and I underwent a major re-organization within the church we attended at the time, and started the process of moving forward to partnering with another one of larger churches in the area. Through several meetings and gatherings over a three month period, I met a girl by the name of Jen Cullinane. Totally didn't think anything of it. Two weeks before Christmas, we partnered with the larger church in feeding families in the area by delivering them Christmas dinners that the families otherwise would not have been able to afford themselves. And in one of the lines where individuals were to pick up their families addresses, I saw Aly. I didn't recognize her right away. Her hair was longer and truth be told I didn't have my glasses on, but soon enough, I knew it was her. So after that, I got to thinking more, "Wait are Jen and Aly related?" Sure enough, I totally Instagram researched, and low and behold, Aly was married to Jen's brother. What are the odds right? I was stoked that Aly was a Jesus girl. I love people in general, but women in business and being a Jesus girl, jackpot! That's like my #highvibetribe!

A couple more weeks went by and one Sunday morning, I was praying, thinking and simply talking with God, "Lord, I need one more person for the book. Just one more interview and I have no clue who it should be. I want it to be someone of influence, someone who is a Jesus girl and a total chic business woman at the same time." And almost immediately Aly popped into my head. I thought, well, the only way I can contact her is via Facebook, so I did. Within minutes she responded right back and was so excited at the opportunity to be featured. The story gets a little a better. I hopped into the car with my kids shortly after my conversation with Aly, headed over to church that Sunday morning, feeling good that I had secured my last interview. I hurried to get inside (all you moms know the drama with getting kids ready and out of the house) and what do you know? I see Jen, Aly's her sister-in-law, up on stage giving her testimony to hundreds of people on how Jesus had changed her life. Forty-eight hours later, I had the privilege of sitting down with Aly over a cup of Starbucks coffee, doing the interview and just getting to know her. She is so full of life and such a smart, savvy business woman. In my mind, anyone who can handle "The Sharks" can pretty much handle anything.

So it gives me great pleasure to introduce you to Mrs. Aly Cullinane, President, of Mrs. Pickles, mom of two little ones and featured on the season five opener of *Shark Tank.*

Social Media
Instagram: @alycullinane
Facebook: Aly Cullinane
Twitter: @AlyCullinane
Website: www.mrs-pickles.com

When did you realize you were an entrepreneur?
I've always had an entrepreneurial spirit. As a young child, I set up Kool-aid stands every weekend, started a massage parlor in my bathroom, and eventually got my babysitting certification at the age of twelve and started my first "real" company, ABC (Aly's Babysitting Co). I was an over-booked babysitting machine until high school, where I retired my business to focus on sports, campus ministry and academics. After graduation, I earned a bachelor's degree in education, which lead to a career as a second grade teacher right out of college. I love children and teaching, but was nudged by the Lord in a new direction very quickly. I started a pickle company. My husband's great-grandma Toots passed on a secret recipe to all the women in the family for generations. My husband and I are high school sweethearts, and ever since we started dating, I begged for the secret family pickle recipe. It wasn't until we were married seven years later that I learned the recipe and my sister-in-law and I started the pickle company. After just one school year, I gave up the security of a stable paycheck and benefits to take a chance on something I loved and was passionate about. It was one of the hardest yet most rewarding decisions I've ever made!

How are you balancing this all right now? Company expansion, two littles, wife life, etc.?
Lots of wine! No, for real though, it's a struggle. I remind myself daily that no one person can do it all, and to be okay with that. I am a perfectionist. If I take on too many responsibilities beyond my core obligations, I end up doing everything (mothering, wifey duties, keeping up with the housework, business, volunteering, mentoring, etc...) at less than 100%,

which doesn't help me reach my goals and overall makes me feel unsuccessful. Overcommitting myself is something I struggle with daily. I have a hard time saying no. I know I am not the only one with this weakness. Am I right, ladies? A strategy that has really helped me to refocus my priorities is to write a weekly to-do/goal list, as well as a daily one before the day even starts. This list incorporates my business duties. This is not an all-inclusive of what I will/want to get done, this is a must-do list. No negotiations, no procrastination. That way, if someone emails or calls me with something they need and it doesn't fit in my five things, sorry it will be done tomorrow. No guilt! I love lists! I am very visual, so seeing these things each morning helps me to stay focused, and therefore spend less time WASTING time!

I keep this list to five things *only*. It doesn't seem like a lot, but they are the "must" things that need to get done. That is how I keep myself accountable as a stay-at-home, work-from-home mom. With these to-do's on my mind, I plan my schedule around my kids, as I don't want them to feel the burden of my workload. I want my kids to stay kids as long as humanly possible! So much so, that I carve out my time with them as a "meeting" in my phone calendar, so that I am not tempted to schedule or do anything else during that time. No checking emails, no answering calls; just like I am in the most important meeting of my career. Let's be real, our kids ARE the most important meeting (a truly divine appointment!). I get up earlier than them to ensure things are done, and stay up late if there are lingering duties. All in all, keep the list short so your feeling of accomplishment/morale stays high. We are all in this together, ladies!

OMG— okay so tell me the story about *Shark Tank*. I am a huge fan of the show and I am dying to know!
It was truly a once in a lifetime experience! It was a couple of years in terms of the process. When we started the company in 2011, everyone kept telling us how much they loved the pickles and asked why we weren't already on *Shark Tank*. We agreed, as it seemed like the most natural thing to do to expand the business. We have a unique product, and a great family history to it. It was really more of people saying, "why not?" It wasn't until we were on our way home from a long day of production in Oregon when we finally got the call from the producers. It couldn't have been better timing. When we first applied, we were nowhere near ready to go on the show, even though we thought we were. It was truly a blessing and God's perfect timing that things evolved the way they did. Not only were we ready business-wise, I was finally ready to start the process of overcoming my fear of public speaking (this is still in the works!)

It was about a three-month process from that first call to going down to LA to film, and in that three months, every time the phone rang, every time there was something new we had to do, it was all prefaced with the phrase "just as a reminder, you could be cut at any point." It's tough to think and hear that as the first sentence out of the gate at every phone call, but we had to just push past the fear of failing and give it to God. The doubts that initially clouded my mind about appearing on national television in front of eight million people could have been enough to waive the white flag. With God in the center of my business, I knew that He would be in the tank with me. Before entering the tank, my business partner and I prayed together, gave it to God, put our matching aprons and high heels on and walked down the hallway into the Shark Tank with a clear mind and a peaceful heart. It was honestly such a calm moment! To this day, I still have people ask me, "have you heard of the show *Shark Tank*? You should totally be on it!"

So you get on the show but, the part that you really got nervous about was actually seeing the replay?
Yes! It's all about the editing. We were in the "tank" for about an hour, and we only got 5-6 minutes of air-time. There was so much footage for them to choose from, and with all you hear about reality TV, (think Bachelor, Real Housewives, etc.) I was a nervous wreck! I knew what I had said in the tank, and was confident in that, it was just a matter of how they would cut and paste. Praise Jesus that we were shown in a very positive light and given a great cut of footage!

What was it like meeting the "Sharks" in person?
It was surprisingly anti-climatic. What you see on TV is exactly what happens. You don't get to chit-chat. They are right down to business. It isn't personal, it's business. You can tell the moments where they are trying to stir up content or controversy for TV. They are very authentic and speak their minds, which is good if they have positive feedback, and obviously bad if they rip your business apart. It is part of the gamble of presenting to the sharks! You become shark bait! Besides Mr. Wonderful not wanting "pickles in his portfolio," we really felt the sharks were nice to us and very constructive with their advice. Barbara was the last shark

in, and definitely the shark we connected with the most. I admire her as a woman and an entrepreneur, so her telling us that we reminded her of herself at our age, was flattering to say the least! Her advice to not take an investment meant a lot, and gave us the reassurance that we were going to be okay without a shark on our team.

Biggest take away from *Shark Tank*?
Definitely Barbara's words of wisdom. The fact that she believed in us to do it on our own was super encouraging. We had dozens of inquires from investors after the show aired, but Barbara's recommendation to re-invest and grow slowly and organically has kept my business, literally, to myself. For that, I am thankful!

How do you see yourself as Jesus would see you?
Oh jeeeez….I hope he would see me as compassionate and fair both in my family life and business. I strive to be just like Him. I am actively working on being a good listener. I make it a point to ask for advice from and listen to others in my field. When others give me words of wisdom, I take those things and ask myself how that would look in my business. God made us all with unique special talents and traits, and my goal when I meet someone is to tap into their strengths and learn from them. I meet people where they are. Everyone is in a different place in their lives. Meet them where they need to met. It brings out the best in people.

Do you have a mission/vision statement?
To bring families around America closer together through our family's traditions, one gourmet pickle at a time.

What inspires you the most in your entrepreneurial journey?

People! I love learning from others. Every week something that I do that keeps me motivated is "Motivational Mondays" where I carve out time to watch a Ted talk, read an inspirational/self-help book, and write out and re-write out all my goals. Time to sit down and think. It's healthy. My pastor sends me content as well, which is always Jesus-led and encouraging. I try to always talk to God and ask where He wants me in the business and where he wants me to go. In the midst of the to-do's it is easy to forget God as my business partner. I make a conscious effort to keep Him at the center. I am always learning, always evolving. A quote that often comes to mind is, "Start where you are. Use what you have. Do what you can." (Arthur Ashe)

What fears do you have and how have or do you overcome those?

I have fear of failure every day, but I am learning as I go how to harness it. Fear itself isn't bad, but if you let it overtake your life and major decisions, you will never gain momentum and move forward with your goals. No two days are the same with business. Since I am managing 100% of everything from accounting, distribution, production, etc., it all falls on my shoulders. When I make decisions, I always get a little scared, thinking, "was that the right decision? Is that going to cost me my business?" I make a lot of mistakes, but that is part of being an entrepreneur. I overcome the fears by choosing what I believe the best path to be, and whether it works out or not, I have gained knowledge. I also talk to Jesus about it. I talk to Him because without

Him I wouldn't even have a business. I consult with similar businesses that have gone before me in my field. I am not afraid to ask questions. I think being honest with your struggles is a good thing too. It's encouraging to remember that everyone has hard times, even Jesus! By asking for help with problems/fears, I often find someone I trust that can offer alternative solutions and a fresh perspective!

What advice do you have for women who may be struggling with hanging on to their WHY?

Definitely find someone who is in the same industry as you. It really does help. Be honest with the struggle as I said before. I would also ask "what is the end goal"? If you don't know that, then you probably don't know why you are doing what you are doing to begin with. I know why I am doing what I am doing, and I keep that at the top of my mind. My goal right now is to be with my kids while they are young. If you are quitting your job to start your own business, why is that? To get away from the 9-5? To finally be passionate about what you do? It may be a combination of things, but when you remind yourself why you are doing it, it will motivate you to keep unfolding the HOW. I definitely am not an expert on how, as I struggle daily, but by keeping the WHY at the front of my mind, it motivates me to keep trying! Dig deep and befriend others with the same "WHY." You are stronger, smarter and more capable than you can imagine.

What is the number one thing you have learned as a Jesus girl in business?

Loaded question......patience, honestly! I think as an entrepreneur, especially as a woman, we want to be good at *everything*. We want everything done in a certain way and in our own time (I am totally type A). Truth of the matter is, things that we want to be done, that we work so hard to do, may not come full circle right away, but that's when Jesus comes in! It all comes in His timing. From the beginning, I chose Jesus to be my business partner. Jesus already works 24/7, so He's a good one to have around for those late nights and early mornings! Being a one-woman team can and is overwhelming at times. I have to remind myself daily that Jesus is right alongside me on this crazy ride, and to trust Him. Doors closing are often not understood until the next door opens. Be patient and you will see that God's plan for you is much bigger than you can comprehend. It may not look like much while you are putting the pieces together, but throughout the puzzle, Jesus will continue to reveal things and opportunities that you never thought were possible, creating a beautiful masterpiece!

What is one thing you do every single day?

I think one thing women in general struggle with is time alone. We do everything for everyone, and with a smile! As much as I love people and serving them (especially those little ones), having that time to myself to think and pray is critical to my health and wellbeing. I'm not talking about folding laundry alone, although that would be nice, too! I make it a point to do a devotional of some sort every day. Honestly, sometimes it is only ten minutes, but I need that time. After I read it, I pray about it, and then ask God how I can apply it to my life. How can I implement this teaching into my home/business/relationships? I start my day with a positive and encouraging attitude to pass on to those around me. Optimism is contagious!

Can you see why this girl totally needed to be featured? What an amazing story. We as women have so many responsibilities. We have so many people that need us, rely on us and in the end, that is such a blessing, *especially* when you are a fierce female entrepreneur. We get so tied up and bogged down with having to do it all, but we fail to realize that God really has everything under control. He is the one that takes care of everything. He fills in the gaps where we cannot do it ourselves. That's the point. We need Jesus in every aspect of our lives. Everything we have, everything we own is not ours. It all belongs to Him and we are here to take care of it and steward it to the best of our abilities. And, ladies, we can't beat ourselves up over not being able to get it all done. In everything, there is a season. Embrace where you are right where you are now. The journey itself is the most important.

Coffee Thoughts:

1. What are some ways you can get fierce with the important things that need to be prioritized?

____

____

____

____

____

2. What are you going to give over to God, so he can take care of the rest?

____

____

____

____

____

3. What are you going to stop *immediately* beating yourself up over?

____

____

____

____

____

CHAPTER 10

THE FINAL CHAPTER OF THE OLD, FIRST CHAPTER OF THE NEW.

"Life is a like a book. Some chapters are sad, some are happy and some are exciting, but if you never turn the page, you will never know what the next chapter has in store for YOU."

–Unknown

End of one, beginning of another

I debated over and over again about including this last chapter in the book. After a lot of prayer and toggling back and forth I decided to include it. The reason I did is because it is my story. And although I will not get into massive details, you will find out why toward the end of this chapter.

As you already know, I spent twelve years in the thick of corporate America. I spent many years living in the pits of depression and anxiety; among many other feelings of inadequacies. I wrestled with the whole Proverbs 31 woman, the perfect wife, the flawless mother, the Pastor's wife identity and I am happy to say that God has both delivered and healed me from all of the hurt, the pain, the struggles, the long nights of crying and weeping and the feelings of being lost and lonely. None of those thoughts and feelings are from God. I ended a twelve-year chapter of my life where the enemy had a major hold on me in more ways than one. There are parts of my story that I have shared with a few people, but never everything all at once. Never in depth or in great detail. I am happy and proud to announce that I am already working on book number two for you all. It will be a twelve-year story of struggle and triumph. A story of deliverance and healing and hope for those that may be living in the depths of depression, anxiety, feelings of inadequacies, points of pain and hurt (both from self and others) and living a life you think you aren't meant to live. It's my story.

It will be an entire tell all. I felt for the longest time, the Holy Spirit tugging on my heart and soul to *bare it all.* It is the last and final step in true freedom......to release it. It may be the only *Jesus* a girl or woman will ever see. And I speak best when I write. Every one of us has a story. But my hope and prayer is that through my own struggles, pain, heartbreak and healing, you, too, will see what Jesus has done in my life, how I am no different than anyone else, but that I just have a Savior who loves me enough to cover me in grace and mercy. To allow me to live out my hopes and dreams after twelve years. For the longest time, I thought, "Wow, twelve years. That seems like a crazy long time." But God had to have me go through it in order to live to tell it, and help those who are going through it and how teach them how to get to the other side.

For my own amusement, I did some research on the significance of the number twelve in the Bible. I felt so ashamed for so long that my time spent in the valley was a twelve-year stint, but after doing the research, here is what I found out about the significance of the number twelve.

The number twelve can be found in 187 places of God's word. The meaning of "12," which is considered a perfect number, is a number that symbolizes God's power and authority. It symbolizes completeness or "the nation of Israel." Christ chose twelve men to bear witness to what he did and spread the good news of the gospel. Our place in Heaven, the New Jerusalem, (will) contain twelve gates made of pearl which are each manned by an angel.

There is so much more I could go into detail about in my research, but when I started to really read what God's Word had to say about it, I knew that I knew God had purpose to my pain. It was no accident in terms of the time I spent during that twelve year period getting real and getting fierce with God. And now….it's time to share that experience, in its fullness and in its completeness.

But before I end this absolutely phenomenal project, I will leave you with my own interview. It is a small snapshot of what is coming in the future.

Social Media
Periscope: @gretchenbarocio
Instagram: @iamthegirlpreneur
Twitter: @gretchenbarocio
Facebook: Gretchen Barocio
SnapChat: @girlpreneur
Website: www.thegirlpreneur.com

So tell us about you!
Well, I am a wife to a super hot worship Pastor at our local church here in the Pacific Northwest. I am a mother of two, a full time entrepreneur, network marketer, author and teacher. I run a brand called #thegirlpreneur, which is a lifestyle brand and connects female entrepreneurs with their God-given potential. Through my experience in business and my passion for entrepreneurship, I am blessed to live the life that God has called me to live.

When did you realize you were an entrepreneur?
I would say that I wasn't necessarily ever sure I was an entrepreneur as much as I was confident I was meant for business. I am absolutely obsessed with business and networking. I think mostly because I love to crunch numbers and meet people. Seems like very opposite ends of the spectrum, but with my husband being a worship Pastor, we are always meeting people. I love people, getting to know them and what

makes them tick. I value deep relationships. I don't do well with surface-y relationships. I have a lot of acquaintances, but my inner circle is so precious. I love my tribe and I love them hard. And in my tribe, we just love doing business and working with people. That's what we do. We change life.

How are you balancing it all right now? Mom, wife of a Pastor, business, etc.?
Yikes. Well, a lot of times I don't. I think it's natural for most women to feel like they need to. I let that plague me for so long (among other things) that it almost destroyed me. But I realize that planning is my BFF. Like seriously. I never say "YES" to anything without checking my calendar. I never overcommit either. I lived in that world for a long time as well, but now, I am so comfortable with saying "NO" to certain things so I can say "YES" to better things. As an entrepreneur, you have to protect that time like it's money because in a very real way, it is. Time is a huge investment and one you can never get back. Be very strategic with where you make your investments in time and where those "deposits" are being made.

Many times, it is easy to get caught up in wanting to make everyone happy. And you just can't. Even Joyce Meyer says, "10% of all people will just not end up liking you, anyway." That's just the way it is. Once I let go of trying to make everyone happy, I started to see things differently. I didn't have the "weight" of others' opinions holding me down. And last time I checked, other people's opinions aren't paying my bills.

How do you see yourself as Jesus would see you?
Well.......*now* I see myself as girl who is perfect in my imperfections. I don't have to be perfect and I don't expect other people to be either. I used to get hung up on perfection, especially being a Pastor's wife. But the beauty is, I don't have to be. Jesus took care of all of that for me. I see myself as a woman who God has called to lead other women through the avenue of business. Ministry is all around us.... not just in the four walls of a church. What is most important in kingdom work is what happens outside of those four walls. How am I treating the barista at Starbucks who jacked up my coffee? How am I treating the person in front of me at the grocery store who is taking forever to write a check? How am I interacting with my children and what am I teaching them? How am I loving that person that spoke slanderous words about me? You have to love like Jesus.......and sometimes, that is just down right hard, but I hope He would see me as a person who really does try to love unconditionally.

Do you have a mission/vision statement?
"Connecting people with potential" is my vision statement. I am a firm believer in that a vision statement and mission statement are two very different things. My mission statement changes as God presses different things on my heart. My vision statement has always been connecting people with potential, but right now my mission is very much working with other female entrepreneurs specifically, and connecting them with their God given potential. You can have Jesus and business. In fact, you *need* Jesus *in* your business as far as I am concerned.

Everyone has their own belief system and that's okay. I just believe Jesus and God have to be the CEO of my business and my life, otherwise, I am no good in my own niche.

What fears do you have and how do you (or did you) overcome them?
Honestly, I don't think fear ever really goes away. Joyce Meyer always says, "New level, new devil." I believe that to be 100% true. I have fear all the time, but the difference with me now versus twelve years ago is that I recognize the enemy at his onset. I just get real with the fear and then refuse to believe it. I really speak it out loud that I refuse to believe the lies of the enemy. Sometimes, actually I am sure always, when people see me in my car driving I am sure they are thinking, "What the heck is that chick doing yelling at herself?" That is usually just me getting real with it, staring that fear in the face and saying, "NOPE." So I am not sure there is a really good answer to that question because I have fears daily, even still. I just learned (the hard way) to get Jesus involved immediately instead of way down the line. I don't have time for the enemy and his games. I have a job to do.

What advice do you have for women who may be struggling with their WHY?
Ohhhh boy. Well, my husband can certainly attest to this. Now, let me be clear and say that my husband is 1000% in support of any and everything I have ever done in my business career, but that doesn't always mean he understands it. Those are two very different concepts.

First, I always go to God, although I didn't used to (especially when my husband didn't understand. Big mistake, don't do that!) There is no point in trying to fight that battle by yourself, let me just be real with you right now on that. You just won't win that battle alone…..ever. You have to get God involved. I am convinced that God did not give me the desires and dreams of my heart for them to just go to waste. He didn't hard wire me the way He did in vain. There was purpose behind it. What I failed to do in the previous twelve years that I am doing now is, I get Him involved right away. If I know deep down that my gut is telling me something (really the Holy Spirit telling what to do) but my husband may not understand, I pray that God work on his heart to help him understand it or help me understand if it's not where I am really supposed to go (because that can happen too.)

Second, I fight for that WHY. I fight hard. I read a lot of positive quotes, inspirational articles, etc. If I feel my mind going down the negative road, I immediately stop and re-read my goals, look over my vision boards again, I say out loud what I wait in expectation from God. I never stop taking action either. That is exactly what the enemy wants me to do. To stop growing and stop taking action. I have lost so many friends following the call on my life. But I'd rather follow the call then have to answer to why I disobeyed the call when I get to the gates of Heaven. Again, it was a hard twelve-year lesson I had to learn. I am no good in the driver's seat of life.

Third, I surround myself with positive propaganda every single day. I don't watch TV. We have TVs, but we only watch what we can stream on Netflix, Hulu, YouTube, etc. TV is complete garbage and brings nothing good into my house. I am also very careful about what I view on my social media feeds. If it's negative, it goes. If it makes me feel bad, ignites unGodly emotions or bitter thinking, it goes. Period. Letting someone, something negative or some crazy rant on social media into your mind is as insane as letting someone come into your home and yell or rant at you in person. You wouldn't normally let someone physically come into your house and yell at you, so why would you do that on social media? Makes no sense to me. That is why God invented the "unfriend" and "unfollow" button.

What is the number one thing you have learned as a Jesus girl in business?

Oh, sheesh, patience. Like seriously. Business is merely people exchanging goods and services. If you don't have patience and people skills, entrepreneurship will eat you alive (which is why you need Jesus *more than ever* in your business). People are people. Hurting people hurt people. You may be on the receiving end of someone's bad day that you had nothing do with, yet they may take it out on you anyway. Meet them at their level. I believe Jesus would have done the same.

What is one thing you do every single day?

Take time to say "Thank You" to God every single day, sometimes for only one thing or sometimes for many things. I would love to say I am in prayer for hours or that I have set daily devos, but I don't. But my attitude of gratitude is extremely important to me and I never want to take for granted what I have.

I have coffee every.....single......day. I can't even talk to most people until I have coffee. And I am okay to say that is probably a little ridiculous, but hey, it's the truth.

Coffee Thoughts:

1. What is the number one thing you have ***now*** learned as a Jesus girl in business?

____
____
____
____
____

2. What chapter can you start to close so you can open the next chapter God has in store for you?

____
____
____
____
____

3. How do you now see yourself as Jesus sees you?

____
____
____
____
____

A FINAL COFFEE THOUGHT

To my fierce females,

You have the power to live a *Fiercely You* lifestyle. You are perfect in the way you have been created and your gifts are unmatched. Harness them, use them, develop them and then, share them with the world.

If you have ever battled with the insecurities of being a Jesus girl in business, have ever thought about being an entrepreneur and don't know if you have what it takes, it is my hope and prayer that you have found it here in *Fiercely You*. I hope that if you have ever felt lost or asked the question '*what is this Jesus thing?*', that you have walked away with a better idea of just how special you are to Him. I pray that if you've ever felt alone in your journey that you've found something new to be hopeful for. And more than anything, I pray that you feel supported, loved, encouraged and reignited about your passions and dreams that may have been dormant for all these years.

I encourage you to keep this book within an arm's reach, so that any time you are feeling like you can't do it or you feel the pressures of the world around you and aren't sure if someone or something is there for you; you can pick this up again in those times and know you aren't alone. I want every fierce female to know that God has the most incredible promises for your life. Understand that He wants nothing more than to bring your hopes and dreams to fruition. Finally, know that I am cheering for you one hundred percent of the time.

And last but not least, if you feel so inclined, please share *Fiercely You* with any female you know that has put the Louboutins back in the closet and could use this to brush the dust of those heels and live life again.

The highest of blessing to you,

Gretchen

CHEERS!

To my husband, Aaron. There are not enough words to express my thanks, gratitude, love and support throughout my journey. You are my number one fan, the love of my life and the perfect person God could have ever blessed me with. I am honored to be your wife. Thank you for always believing in me and championing me in the most perfect of ways.

To my parents, for always instilling in me the true essence of hard work, perseverance and what true success is made of. I learned entrepreneurship from the best.

To the nine #JesusGirls who were gracious enough to share their stories of struggle and triumph....you will never know just how much you have impacted my life. I blessed and humbled that you have shared your life stories with the world.

To my fabulous life coach, Cara Alwill Leyba. Outside of my family, you believed in me before I believed in myself. The impact you have had on my life is incredible. You are the Chanel of the industry my dear. Simply the best.

To Lisa, I seriously have no clue what I would do without you. Whether you know it or not, you have inspired me to greatness.

To Cara Lockwood, I will cherish the compliment you gave me the first time you ever read this book. I have never received a compliment like that in my life and I am so grateful for your fabulous mind as an editor and helping me with this project.

To Josh Gonzales, founder of x35Creative. You knocked this cover out of the park!

To my readers and viewers, without you......there would be no #GIRLPRENEUR. I am so grateful your support and your words of encouragement. You are the biggest reason I am here to do what I do. If it weren't for you all, I'd just be writing and talking to an iPhone. You are the reason I am here and I am truly blessed by each and every one of you.

ABOUT GRETCHEN BAROCIO

Gretchen Barocio, a Seattle University graduate, is a former Corporate America Executive who spent twelve years working for some of the largest Fortune 500 companies.

Over the last three years she has built a home business partnering with a biotech company that has become the sixth firm in the world to hit the one-billion-dollar mark in under five years. Gretchen is also the founder and creator of the brand #THEGIRLPRENEUR, which is a brand that teaches and empowers female entrepreneurs to build the business of their dreams and be exactly who they were created to be in Jesus.

She is dedicated to working with those who really want change in their business life, achieve a higher level of financial freedom, personal and spiritual excellence. She works to empower each individual to take charge of their circumstances and not to become victims of the circumstance.

> "I am a huge believer that happiness is the precursor to success. I didn't have true happiness until I dug deep into my relationship with Jesus and those around me. As someone who has beaten the odds not only with past health issues, I beat the odds of becoming another statistic in the business world. It is only through Him that I am here today to be able to teach and train others to do the same in their businesses. I became fanatical about my relationship with Jesus and completely obsessed with growing my business and brand for Him. And if I am ever the smartest person in the room, I know I am in the wrong room. I am a life long learner. You have to take life and get fierce with it."
>
> —Gretchen Barocio

Gretchen resides in the Pacific Northwest with her husband Aaron, who is a worship Pastor for their local church, and her two sons Isaac and Levi.

16150985R00100

Printed in Great Britain
by Amazon